EARLY TUDOR CRITICISM
Linguistic and Literary

EARLY TUDOR CRITICISM

Linguistic & Literary

BY ELIZABETH J. SWEETING

> The resonabyll manns imagynashyon
> Joynd w[ith] resonabyll consyderacyon
> Bryngth man muche pleseur in consyderyng
> The pleasant proporte of eche pleasaunt thyng
> Possessyd to man's behof at comandyng.
>   JOHN HEYWOOD, *Wytty and Wyttles.*

New York
RUSSELL & RUSSELL
1964

FIRST PUBLISHED IN 1940
REISSUED, 1964, BY RUSSELL & RUSSELL, INC.
BY ARRANGEMENT WITH BASIL BLACKWELL, OXFORD
L. C. CATALOG CARD NO: 64—15043

PRINTED IN THE UNITED STATES OF AMERICA

CONTENTS

Chap.		Page
	Prefatory Note	ix
	Introduction	xi
I.	The Earliest Tudor Phase	1
II.	The Translation of the Bible	23
III.	Secular Translation and Translators	42
IV.	Education: Tutor and Schoolmaster	58
V.	The Universities	87
VI.	Rhetoric and Literary Criticism	107
VII.	Early Tudor Drama	125
VIII.	Irony and Parody ; The New Courtly Poetry	154
	Conclusion	170
	Index	173

PREFATORY NOTE

THIS preliminary survey of critical activity is intended to cover the period extending from the late fifteenth century to the accession of Elizabeth. The preservation of critical material during the Middle Ages must be a separate study; only general references, therefore, have been made to the earlier period where it seemed necessary to notice a parallel or indicate preparation for later developments. Elizabeth's accession seems to provide a natural limit, since first- and second-hand material for the study of Elizabethan criticism is readily accessible. It is the principal object of this book to map out the lines of preparation and advance which activate the Elizabethan material widely known through such collections as Gregory Smith's *Elizabethan Critical Essays*.

This study of early Tudor criticism was undertaken as a thesis for the degree of Master of Arts in the University of London. It was successfully presented in June 1938 and was recommended for publication. A brief Conclusion has been added; otherwise, in the course of a thorough revision for the Press, it has been my aim to condense the wording wherever possible and to simplify the documentation. I am grateful to the Governors of the Royal Holloway College and to the University of London for the award of the Katherine Block and other studentships which gave the sinews of research. It is a pleasant duty also to acknowledge the financial assistance to which I owe the opportunity to publish, notably from the Publication Fund of the University of London. Professor A. W. Reed stimulated my work by his interest and many others have given me the benefit of their wider scholarship and experience. Above all, I wish to express my gratitude to Miss G. D. Willcock, whose unfailing help and encouragement have accompanied me every step of the way.

INTRODUCTION

THAT effective English criticism is a mid-sixteenth century invention and the result of the Revival of Learning is implicit or explicit in more than one standard work of reference on the subject. The crucial importance for the sixteenth-century mind of the recovery of classical texts is, of course, undeniable, as a large proportion of the following pages must testify, but the limits within which the leaven of 'Humanism' worked effectively, the variations in resistance and response not only in different social and cultural layers but in different decades (since later periods do not always prove more permeable than earlier) are being increasingly recognized. It is important to gauge accurately the strength of the mediaeval inheritance, persisting in certain fields, not by the passive toughness of inertia but by innate liveliness. It is true that before the mid-Tudor period 'not a single critical treatise on English existed in the English language or even in Latin'[1] but wherever there is in the world of letters a sense of change, a recognition of comparisons and contrasts, wherever there are incentives to controversy, there will be exercise of the critical faculty, whether or not any codified principles emerge. The nearest approach to critical utterance before the sixteenth century has been found in Caxton's '*naïf* and interesting, but only infantilely critical, remarks'[2] in his prefaces. The suggestion of childish first steps here is misleading, for the bulk of Caxton's critical *dicta* find their place in a critical tradition well-rooted in the mediaeval past and by no means destined to wither under sixteenth-century conditions.

Criticism can be considered in two main orders, which may be termed the 'static' and the 'dynamic.' The 'static' is the measuring aspect, the application to literature and language of inherited and accepted standards. This function

[1] George Saintsbury, *History of English Criticism* (1911), p. 28.   [2] *Ibid.*

INTRODUCTION

was served in the Middle Ages by rhetoric and grammar, surviving in the encyclopaediae which were then the chief sources of classical knowledge.[1] Models for the application of these rules were to be found in such classical literature as had escaped the general wreck of culture. The value of the encyclopaedists is proved by the fact that Petrarch, living on the threshold of a new age, mentions Isidore of Seville, one of the most widely-known of them, as a source of poetic theory[2] and that they continued to be printed and read side by side with the work of more enlightened writers during the fifteenth and sixteenth centuries. The study of rhetoric and grammar preserved almost unchanged a formal code of rules applicable to both language and literature from the classical period to the regeneration of learning in the sixteenth century. From their use and application arise the large number of 'arts of poetry' which discuss subtlety and appropriateness of diction, literary forms, the differences between prose and poetic styles and other matters which belong to the domain of critical theory. Through the ages during which the arts were the handmaidens of theology, these works cultivate attention to literary creation and preserve it as an independent art.

These activities, however, could work only within certain limits during the Middle Ages. The supply and circulation of classical literature were very restricted. Such manuscripts as survived were laboriously copied by hand, and, although there were individual foundations in which this industry flourished, the supply was quite inadequate. When, during the twelfth century with the rise of the universities, copying became almost a trade, classical literature was swamped by the spate of scholastic work. The next century was marked by the eager quest and recovery in Italy of manuscripts which had long remained forgotten in remote libraries and

[1] See P. Abelson, *The Seven Liberal Arts* (Columbia University Teachers' College Contributions to Education, No. 11, 1906).
L. J. Paetow, *The Arts Course at Mediaeval Universities* (University of Illinois Studies, Vol. III, No. 7, 1910).
[2] See J. H. Robinson and H. W. Rolfe, *Petrarch* (1914), p. 263.

INTRODUCTION

monasteries. During the fifteenth century, Englishmen studying in Italy were fired by the enthusiasm of Italian collectors and patrons of letters and brought many important manuscripts back for university and private libraries. Thus new stores of knowledge and new methods of study were opened up to the scholars of the generation of Humphrey, Duke of Gloucester, and the succeeding one.[1] Their mental horizon was widened and they caught a glimpse of the scholarship which 'eventually means criticism, the discipline of exact thinking within a certain field.'[2]

The second order of criticism, which may be called the 'dynamic,' consists in debate and controversy, the raising of new questions, the polishing of old intellectual weapons and the forging of new. In the Middle Ages the dynamic force of criticism was supplied by linguistic controversies. The vernaculars of Europe were striving to free themselves from the ignoble position in the hierarchy of languages to which they had been relegated. A knowledge of Latin was the key to the *corpus* of classical knowledge, to the universal medium of scholars and of the Church, while the vernaculars were in comparison unstable and considered unfit for serious purposes.

In England the vernacular had a dual task to accomplish. Before it could prove itself equal to much of the expressive power which was assumed to be the prerogative of Latin, it had to emerge from its eclipse by the language of the Norman invaders and its degradation as the tongue of a conquered people. While Latin was the *sine qua non* of the scholar, French was the aristocratic language, and it was the aim of every ambitious Englishman to use it as one to the manner born. Nevertheless, the eclipse of the English language was only temporary and the struggle for its re-establishment was beginning in the thirteenth century. By the late fourteenth century, when Higden comments on the use of

[1] See K. H. Vickers, *Humphrey, Duke of Gloucester* (1907).
[2] J. S. Phillimore, 'Thomas More and the Arrest of Humanism in England,' *Dublin Review* (July and October 1913).

INTRODUCTION

English in schools,[1] a generation was being trained to the familiar use of English instead of French. Although there remained a few who

> wol lykne hamsylf to gentil men, and fondeþ wiþ gret bysynes for to speke Freynsch, for to be more ytold of,[2]

even the upper classes had begun to use English for personal letters.[3] At the same time as French was yielding to English in familiar uses, Latin was giving way in the more conservative spheres of law and commerce. So already by the late fifteenth century the language had weathered a period of strain and stress and had become a nexus of comment, criticism and debate.

There were, however, unruly and diverse elements within the language itself to be reconciled. It was a serious drawback to the prestige of English that 'þe burþ-tonge of Englysch men, and here oune longage and tonge' should be so 'dyuers of soon in þis yland'.[4] Until some approach to uniformity had been made it could have no standard speech for literary purposes. It was fortunate for the future of the language that the bulk and excellence of Chaucer's work provided the necessary stabilisation. For succeeding generations the London dialect in which he chose to write became the most conformable and readily used. As well as determining the future choice of language, he provides the link between the literary knowledge of the Middle Ages and the wealth of new material which was beginning to flow in from the Continent. He was familiar with the poetical

---

[1] *Polychronicon*, Trevisa's translation: '... now, þe ȝer of oure Lord, a þousand þre hondred foure score & fyue, ... in al the gramerscoles of England children leueþ Frensch, and construeþ and lurneþ an Englysch.' (K. Sisam, *Fourteenth Century Verse and Prose*, 1921, p. 149.)
[2] *Ibid.*, pp. 148–149.
[3] See C. L. Kingsford, *Prejudice and Promise in Fifteenth Century England* (1925).
R. C. Anderson, 'Letters of the Fifteenth and Sixteenth Centuries from the Archives of Southampton,' *Publications of Southampton Record Society* (1921).
R. W. Chambers, *On the Continuity of English Prose*, an extract, published separately, from the Introduction to Nicholas Harpsfield's Life of Sir Thomas More, ed. E. V. Hitchcock and R. W. Chambers, E.E.T.S. (1932).
[4] Trevisa, *op. cit.*, p. 148.

xiv

INTRODUCTION

devices handed down by the art of rhetoric[1] and put new life into English poetry by his judicious adoption of anything in French and Italian literature which could be happily combined with native stock. He had a facility in establishing contacts, an awareness of outside influences and the ability to make wise critical decisions. It proves the alertness of the Early Tudor interest in language that in the long line of eulogy which appeared in the fifteenth and early sixteenth centuries strong emphasis is always laid on his services to the language, ranking him among those

> faders dere
> That lyston our language to enhaunce.[2]

In an age which tended to value the florid in diction Chaucer is praised for his language

> so fayr and pertynente
> It semeth unto mannys heerynge
> Not only the word but verely the thynge.[3]

Appreciation of language is a strong link between the age of Chaucer and one which frequently undervalued mediaeval achievement.

While Chaucer's services to the language are rendered indirectly, because he set the hall mark of literary excellence on a dialect which was becoming important for other and non-literary reasons, in the next generation one of the first conscious critics of language appeared. Reginald Pecock is remarkable for his careful consideration of a problem which was hotly debated in the Early Tudor period, concerning the kind of language most suitable for devotional works. He realized that Bible study might be a dangerous thing if the language were such as to admit of misunderstanding. Thinking the language had too many foreign and Latin formations, he attempted to replace these by Saxon com-

---

[1] See J. M. Manly, *Chaucer and the Rhetoricians* (Warton Lecture on English Poetry, No. 17, 1926).
[2] Caxton, *Boke of Curtesye*, ed. H. Bradley, E.E.T.S. (Extra Series, 3), 1898, p. 43, ll. 432–434.
[3] *Ibid.*, p. 35.

xv

INTRODUCTION

pounds.[1] Unhappily, his ear for harmonious sentence structure is not equal to his zeal for words and the total effect of his work is one of sesquipedalian clumsiness. The importance of his experiment lies in the spirit in which it was undertaken, the evidence of a striking critical interest in language on the eve of the Early Tudor period.

The succeeding generation produced both personalities and favourable conditions for the fostering of this interest. Caxton helped to guide with sound common sense the early supply of printed books and the selection of texts, catering for the aristocracy and for the mass of ordinary people who, since the advent of printing, formed a new and avid reading public. Scholarly circles discussed and formulated new ideals, problems of language assumed new importance in the debates on translation, Biblical and secular, educational systems were examined and revised. This vigour and variety of debate must have proved useful in any case. It gained power and effectiveness from the fact that it found driving force and a unifying factor in the eager patriotic consideration of language. Here can be found the clear lines of what amounts to a critical programme, continually widening its scope to include topics later to be considered purely literary. This is the critical tradition and programme passed on to Elizabethan letters by writers like Ascham and Wilson. Only by an appreciation of its range and tenacity can the true place in the Elizabethan world of ideas of the 'neo-classic' or Italianate elements be justly appreciated.

[1] See *Donet*, ed. Miss E. V. Hitchcock, E.E.T.S. (Original Series 156), 1921.
Folewer, ed. Miss E. V. Hitchcock, E.E.T.S. (Original Series 164), 1924.
Reule of Crysten Religioun, ed. W. C. Greet, E.E.T.S. (Original Series 171), 1927.

CHAPTER I

THE EARLIEST TUDOR PHASE

THE earliest Tudor phase is a germinal period from both the literary and the linguistic points of view. In the work of Skelton, Hawes and Gavin Douglas among the poets and of Caxton and Lord Berners among the writers of prose, there is a notable capacity to develop and try new things within a mainly mediaeval sphere.

One mode of examining the literary taste of the age is the study of its modifications of allegory, the 'dominant form' of the Middle Ages.[1] The reverence for the aureate language and elaborate forms of Lydgate, as compared with the relative simplicity of Chaucer, proves that the poets of this period still admired

> the guyse / in olde antyquyte
> Of the poetes olde / a tale to surmyse
> To cloke the trouthe / of theyr infyrmyte
> Or yet on Ioye / to haue moralyte ... [2]

Hawes laments the lack of worthy successors to the master of allegory:

> It is to grete truely / me for to tell
> Sythen the tyme / that his lyfe was gone
> In all this realme / his pere dyde no dwell
> Aboue all other / he dyde so excell
> None syth his tyme / art wolde succede
> After theyr deth / to haue fame for theyr mede.
>
> But many a one / is ryght well experte
> In this connynge / but vpon auctoryte
> They fayne no fables / pleasaunt and couerte
> But spend theyr tyme in vaynfull vanyte

---

[1] See C. S. Lewis, *The Allegory of Love* (1936).
[2] Stephen Hawes, *The Pastime of Pleasure*, ed. W. E. Mead, E.E.T.S. (Original Series 173), 1928, p. 6, ll. 51–54. Further references throughout will be to this edition.

EARLY TUDOR CRITICISM

> Makynge balades / of feruent amyte
> As gestes and tryfles / without fruytfulnes
> Thus all in vayne / they spende theyr besynes.[1]

Skelton's allegory, the *Bowge of Courte* (before 1509), is written

> callynge to mynde the greate auctoryte
> Of poetes olde, whyche full craftely,
> Vnder as couerte termes as coude be,
> Can touche a trouth and cloke it subtylly
> Wyth fresshe vtteraunce full sentencyously. . . .[2]

The emphasis in these comments upon the allegorical tradition is always upon the cloaking of meaning in the mists of 'couerte' expression, for the heritage of Lydgate was a distrust of simplicity. The aim of poets is that expressed by Hawes when he avows his intention of following

> the trace / and all the parfytenesse
> Of my mayster Lydgate / with due exercyse.[3]

Hawes, therefore, and Skelton in his allegorical work, accept the tradition of allegory and the aureate language considered appropriate to this *genre*. Up to a certain point they apply the standards set by their chosen master and the artifice by which a web of language is spun. This choice imposes upon them the necessity of working according to the rules of rhetoric, which had maintained all through the Middle Ages a critical apparatus for dealing with diction and style. Hawes, conducting his hero, Grand Amoure, through the Seven Liberal Arts, elaborates the discourse of rhetoric more fully than that of any other art, showing his preoccupation with the machinery of composition. Of 'Ymagynacyon,' the second part of rhetoric, he says:

> Full meruaylous / is the operacyon
> To make of nought / reason sentencyous //
> Clokynge a trouthe / with colour tenebrous
> For often vnder a fayre fayned fable
> A trouthe appereth gretely profytable.[4]

---

[1] *Ibid.*, p. 57, ll. 1387–1393.
[2] *Poetical Works*, ed. A. Dyce (1843), Vol. I, p. 30, ll. 8–12. This edition has been used for all further references.
[3] *Op. cit.*, p. 6, ll. 47–48.   [4] *Ibid.*, p. 33, l. 710–p. 34, l. 714.

THE EARLIEST TUDOR PHASE

Yet, although both Hawes and Skelton accept this method, the finished products are by no means simply reproductions of earlier models, but re-modelled and stamped with the impress of their individual personalities. Hawes is the romantic dreamer, surveying 'faery lands forlorn' in a 'fayre twy lyt.[1] Skelton is the observer and the satirist recognizing, nevertheless, a driving force behind the poet's work. He is sure that there is

> ... a spyrituall,
> And a mysteriall,
> And a mysticall
> Effecte energiall,
> As Grekes do it call
> Of suche an industry,
> And suche a pregnacy,
> Of heuenly inspyracion
> In laureate creacyon,
> Of poetes commendacion,
> That of diuyne myseracion
> God make his habytacion
> In poetes whiche excelles,
> And soiourns with them and dwelles.[2]

Although Hawes says he wishes to produce a Lydgatian allegory, the form he creates is a new one. The didactic purpose is frequently lost to view in his

> perambulat waye / full of all varyaunce[3]

and all his acquaintance with the rules of rhetoric cannot inhibit his pleasure in journeying rather than in arriving. Like Malory he tries to recreate the passing days of chivalry. Grand Amoure has to study courtly feats of arms at the Tower of Chivalry and acquire the knowledge of the Seven Liberal Arts under the guidance of Lady Doctrine.[4] The account of his quest combines the allegory of love with the chivalric romance. This capacity for variation and re-

[1] *Ibid.*, p. 17, l. 328.
[2] *A Replycacyon Agaynst Certayne Yong Scolers Abiured of Late, &c.* Vol. I, p. 222, ll. 365–378.
[3] *Op. cit.*, p. 34, l. 740.
[4] *Ibid.*, p. 24, ll. 503–504.

combination is indicative of a breadth and energy in the age.

While Hawes shifts the emphasis towards a pleasure more purely poetic than didactic in the *Pastime of Pleasure*, Skelton's valuation of Lydgatian allegory is implicit in the gradual discarding of the type as he passes from abstract to concrete and from indirect to direct statement. In the *Bowge of Courte* he uses the framework of allegory, but the action takes place, not in May meadows, but at

<blockquote>
Harwyche Porte, . . .
In myne hostes house, called Powers Keye.[1]
</blockquote>

The figures of the dream, Harry Hafter, with his 'gotyshe berde,' the 'rusty gallande' Ryotte and the rest have more affinity with the characters of *The Visions of Piers the Plowman* than with the tapestry shadows of Lydgate and Hawes. Skelton's fierce satire bursts through the fragile framework of allegory. A vigorous age will find room for contrasting orders of poetry, and in his own mind and world Skelton found ample incentive and scope for the gradual realization of his peculiar gifts.

In *Speke, Parrot* (1517–18) he moves a step farther away from allegory. It becomes in this work a flimsy protection against a charge of treason for his outspoken comments on contemporary learning and politics. His self-eulogy, *The Garlande of Laurell* (composed *c*.1520, published 1523), keeps a framework of allegory, but is too full of unco-ordinated elements to be restrained within this form. The 'aureate' language of the opening and the delicate simplicity of the lyrics to ladies of his acquaintance, the visions of the 'Quene of Fame' and 'Dame Pallas,' the enumeration of his peers in poetic achievement and tributes to his masters are hardly held together. Meanwhile the severance from allegory had become complete in *Colyn Cloute* (*c*.1519). It is a dramatic monologue in vigorous Skeltonics, abandoning the farrago of allegorical devices for plain statement. Colyn says:

[1] *Op. cit.*, Vol. I, p. 31, ll. 34–35.

THE EARLIEST TUDOR PHASE

> I purpose to shake oute
> All my connyng bagge,
> Lyke a clerkely hagge.[1]

and Skelton proceeds in this manner without further preamble or elaboration.

The critical significance of the work of Hawes and Skelton lies in their readiness to make their own valuation of the literary *genres* of their age. The use made by Hawes of the romantic allegory foreshadows the supreme chivalric romance of Spenser and proves Hawes' right to be reckoned among the formative influences of the sixteenth century. Skelton's realist work goes much farther than that of many later Tudor writers. His onset when free from allegory is more directly personal and human. The background of his scholarship is wide. Robert Whittinton praises the ease and elegance of his Latin work[2] and Caxton his skill in translation:

> For he hath late translated the epystlys of Tulle / and the boke of Iyodorus syculus, and diuerse other werkes oute of latyn in to englysshe not in rude // and olde langage. but in polysshed and ornate termes craftely. as he that hath redde vyrgyle / ouyde. tullye. and all the other noble poetes and oratours / to me vnknowen. . . .[3]

He himself cites a comprehensive list of classical authors in the *Garlande of Laurell*, including the rhetoricians, 'olde Quintiliane· with his Declamacyons,' Cicero, 'Prynce of eloquence,' the Greek and Latin poets, 'Theocritus with his bucolycall relacyons,' Virgil 'the Mantuan, with his Eneidos,' Horace 'with his new poetry,' Homer 'the fresshe historian,' Ovid, 'enshryned with the Musis nyne,' the prose writers, Sallust and Livy, the dramatists, Terence and Plautus—all the sources of classical knowledge of this period. His mention of the names of Poggio, Petrarch and

---
[1] *Ibid.*, Vol. I, p. 313, ll. 50–53.   [2] *Op. cit.*, Vol. I, p. xviii, l. 93.
[3] *Eneydos* (1490), Prologue. *The Prologues and Epilogues of William Caxton*, ed. W. J. B. Crotch, E.E.T.S. (Original Series 176), 1928, p. 109. Further references will be to this edition.

EARLY TUDOR CRITICISM

Gaguin shows his acquaintance with later European scholarship. Skelton dissociates himself, however, from the English humanists. No English names, not even those of More and Linacre, occur in the catalogues of the *Garlande of Laurell* or *Phyllyp Sparowe*. He is actively antagonistic to the advancing study of Greek, which was soon to be identified in conservative minds with the incursion of new ideas. The Parrot says,

> In *Academia* Parrot dare no probleme kepe;
> For *Graece fari* so occupyeth the chayre,
> That *Latinum fari* may fall to rest and slepe,
> And *syllogisari* was drowned at Sturbrydge fayre;
>
> Tryuals and quatryuyals so sore now they appayre,
> That Parrot the popagay hath pytye to beholde
> How the rest of good lernyng is roufled vp and trold.[1]

The value of Skelton's work is not increased by any connection with the literary thought of definitely Renascence type. Both Hawes and Skelton show an advance from earlier forms, but the shadow of coming events does not seem to have touched them. Such independent critical faculty as they reveal in their handling of mediaeval forms must be accounted rather to their individual talents and to the spirit of the age in which they were working, a time in which political as well as cultural conditions encouraged both consolidation and enterprise.

Another innovation in poetic form is made by Alexander Barclay's *Eclogues* (*c.* 1530), which mark the adoption of the classical pastoral into English. It is, however, improbable that there is any critical significance in his choice. He seems unconscious of blazing a new trail and to have adopted the eclogue form merely as a convenient one for moralizing on contemporary conditions. The later poets who used the pastoral in the full Tudor period, such as Barnabe Googe and Spenser, made an independent study and choice of model, not looking back to Barclay. Barclay's attention to this form indicates the general broadening of basis in the

[1] *Op. cit.*, Vol. II, p. 8, l. 167–p. 9, l. 173.

THE EARLIEST TUDOR PHASE

Early Tudor period, the variety of literary interests which were growing up.

At the turn of the century and in the early decades of the sixteenth century the character of English literature is very complex. Hawes' use of material from Boccaccio[1] and Barclay's attention to Mantuan and Sallust[2] show a readiness to make use of foreign and classical work. This outward-looking tendency had been found, of course, among Middle English writers wherever they had found in Italy or elsewhere material suitable for their own purposes. Chaucer was indebted to Petrarch and Boccaccio, who had something for all comers. In the late fifteenth century there is felt to be a new stirring of life. After an interval of slower movement the *tempo* quickens. There is increased eagerness to annex whatever may be of interest and value. At the very least, prolixity becomes associated with more fertility and is diversified by some acuteness of perception. In this atmosphere of literary curiosity the critical faculty could be called into being and, true to its mediaeval heritage, is most fully expressed in the linguistic field.

Linguistic discussion is prolific during this period. The literary fashions of the time were superimposed upon a language in which new tendencies were widening the gulf between past and present, thus opposing obstacles to the understanding of literary tradition as well as offering new problems for solution. Chaucer's work had done much to provide a standard literary speech, but since his time further phonological and inflexional changes and changes in vocabulary had taken place in the language. The work of the preceding centuries is therefore felt to be almost as difficult for the writers of the sixteenth century as the remote Anglo-Saxon period. To make Trevisa's translation of Higden's *Polycronicon* comprehensible to his readers Caxton

---

[1] See C. W. Lemmi, 'The Influence of Boccaccio on Hawes' Pastime of Pleasure,' *Review of English Studies*, Vol. V (1929), pp. 195–198.

[2] 'Here begynneth the famous cronycle of the warre which the romayns had agaynst Jugurth usurper of the kyngdome of Numidy: whiche cronycle is compyled in latyn by the renowned romayn Salust. (Published by Pynson between 1519 and 1524.)

finds it necessary to make many alterations in vocabulary. He explains:

> I William Caxton a symple person . . . somewhat haue chaunged the rude and old englyssh / that is to wete certayn wordes / which in these dayes be neither vsyd ne vnderstanden / . . .[1]

Reading an 'olde boke'[2] in search of the 'olde and homely termes',[3] he has been advised to use in his translations, Caxton finds the language quite incomprehensible, for

> . . . certaynly the englysshe was so rude and brood that I coude not wele vnderstande it. And also my lorde abbot of westmynster ded do shewe to me late certayn euydences wryton in olde englysshe for to reduce it in to our englysshe now vsid./ And certaynly it was wreton in suche wyse that it was more lyke to dutche than englysshe I coude not reduce ne brynge it to be vnderstonden.[4]

Whatever may be the date of these 'euydences' all the English of the past is found difficult and drastic changes were felt to have taken place within living memory. Caxton says:

> And certaynly our langage now vsed varyeth ferre from that whiche was vsed and spoken whan I was borne / For we englysshe men / ben borne vnder the domynacyon of the mone. whiche is neuer stedfaste / but euer wauerynge / wexynge one season / and waneth] dyscreaseth another season / . . .[5]

The linguistic flux is complicated also by the diversity of dialects in England where

> that comyn englysshe that is spoken in one shyre varyeth from a nother,[6]

and, even in Kent, so near to London where the standard language was strongest, was

> spoken as brode and rude englissh as is in ony place of englond. . . .[7]

Flourishing beside this uncouth native speech was

---

[1] *Polycronicon* (1482), Bk. VII, Epilogue, *op. cit.*, p. 68.
[2] *Eneydos*, Prologue. *Ibid.*, p. 108.
[3] *Ibid.*   [4] *Ibid.*   [5] *Ibid.*   [6] *Ibid.*
[7] *The Recueil des Histoires de Troyes* (1476), Prologue, leaf 2ᵛ, *op. cit.*, p. 4.

THE EARLIEST TUDOR PHASE

a fashion for elaborate and highly ingenious language, the product of the 'facundious art of Rethorike.'[1] This self-conscious, highly artificial style is all the more important in the training of sixteenth century linguistic interests since the fashion for patterned speech persists in the 'Euphuism' which was one of the most pronounced trends of literary language in the full Tudor period. Berners is, perhaps, the most deliberate stylist of this period and exemplifies linguistic preference consistently maintained. He made his translation of Guevara's *Book of the Emperor, Marcus Aurelius* (1529) from the French version by René Bertaut (1531). The inter-relations of the Spanish and French styles and those of Berners and John Lyly have been much discussed.[2] Whatever these may be, it is certain that the vogue for elaborate speech was current in Europe during this period. It was shared by poets such as the 'rhétoriqueurs' Jean Marot and Jean Lemaire de Belges as well as by the prose writers. Berners uses both the tendencies of that style, the aureation of vocabulary and the patterning of sentences. His response to the rhetorical cult is, however, discriminating, since in his translation he has too much sense of the individuality of his author to impose the elaborate style where it is not appropriate. The preface to his Froissart is in his own rhetorical vein, but the use of plainer style with vigour behind it for the actual translation is a recognition of the spirit of the original. Berners' choice of ornate speech represents the taste of the aristocratic patrons of literature of his day, which is reflected also in the comments of Caxton.

Cultured noblemen stimulated the progress of literature by ordering and supervising translations of their favourite works and by demanding courtly literature of entertainment. Supply of these demands by printers such as Caxton called for the careful exercise of both literary and linguistic

---
[1] Lord Berners, Translator's Prologue to *Arthur of Little Britain* (1524-5), Fol. iii^v.
[2] See W. Landmann, *Das Euphuismus* (1881).
  C. Grifin Child, *John Lyly and Euphuism*. (Münchener Beiträge VII, 1894).
  A. Feuillerat, *John Lyly* (1910).
  V. M. Jeffery, *John Lyly and the Italian Renaissance* (1928).

EARLY TUDOR CRITICISM

judgment. Caxton had to pay due attention to the requests of his influential patrons and work according to their tastes in the polished style which they preferred. There is a section of his work which

> is not requysyte ne eke conuenyent for euery rude and symple man, whiche vnderstandeth not of science ne connyng . . . but for noble / wyse /] grete lordes gentilmen] marchau*n*tes that haue seen] dayly ben occupyed in maters towchyng the publyque weal.[1]

His translation of the *Order of Chyualry* (1484?) is, like Malory's *Morte d'Arthur*, an appeal for the reinstatement of the chivalric ideal and is addressed to the 'Knyghtes of Englond,' whom he asks:

> . . . where is the custome and vsage of noble chyualry that was vsed in the dayes / what do ye now / but go to the baynes] playe atte dyse And some not wel aduysed vse not honest and good rule ageyn alle ordre of knyghthode / leue this / leue it and rede the noble volumes of saynt graal of lancelot / of galaad / of Trystram / of perse forest / of percyual / of gawayn /] many mo. . . .[2]

As well as this literature of courtly instruction Caxton's press provided the romances which were the light reading of the aristocracy, for

> all vertuouse yong noble gentylmen] wymmen for to rede therin as for their passe tyme / . . .' and for 'gentyl yong ladyes] damoysellys. . . .'[3]

Caxton feels himself unequal to the handling of the appropriate ornate language. Deference to the wishes of his noble patrons cannot compel this Kentishman, 'a symple person,'[4] to relinquish his own conviction that plain speech is the best. He willingly acknowledges his lack of instruction in rhetorical models:

> I confesse me not lerned ne knowynge the arte of rethoryk /

[1] *Tullius of Olde Age* (1481), Prohemye, *op. cit.*, pp. 42–43.
[2] Epilogue, *ibid.*, p. 84.
[3] *Blanchardyn and Eglantine* (1489), Prologue, *ibid.*, p. 105.
[4] *Polycronicon*, Bk. VII, Epilogue, *ibid.*, p. 68.

THE EARLIEST TUDOR PHASE

ne of suche gaye termes as now be sayd in these dayes and vsed....[1]

He distrusts the craze for ornamentation which results in obscurity:

> For in these dayes euery man that is in ony reputacyon in his cou*n*tre. wyll vtter his co*m*mynycacyon and maters in suche maners] termes that fewe men shall vnderstonde theym / And som ho-//nest and grete clerkes haue ben wyth me and desired me to wryte the moste curyous termes that I coude fynde / And thus bytwene playn rude /] curyous I stande abasshed.[2]

Caxton's importance as a critic of language lies in his trust in his own independent judgment, his refusal to be harried by his patrons into a cast of speech which is alien to his character and preference. As an Englishman of the southeastern counties he is familiar with the language in its London form and with dialectal variation. As printer and translator he examines older English and foreign languages. Working for aristocratic circles he is *au fait* with all the more fantastic fashions of speech. From all these strata of language he selects the plain style as comprehensible and acceptable for all purposes and thus anticipates at this early date the later judgment of scholars such as Castiglione in Italy, Wilson and Cheke in England. Caxton's judgment is emphatically an independent one. He says, '... in my Iudgemente' when he explains his preference for 'the comyn termes that be dayli vsed'[3] and he consciously tries to find a middle style between the uncouthness of very plain English and the aureate terms:

> ... in a meane bytwene bothe I haue reduced] translated this sayd booke in to our englysshe not ouer rude or curyous but in suche termes as shall be vnderstanden by goddys grace accordynge to my copye.[4]

He anticipates the conviction of the later translators that the opening up of the resources of knowledge to the

---

[1] *Blanchardyn and Eglantine*, ibid., p. 105.
[2] *Eneydos*, Prologue, ibid., pp. 108–109.
[3] *Eneydos*, Preface, ibid., p. 109.   [4] *Ibid.*

EARLY TUDOR CRITICISM

unlearned is 'a noble] a meritorious dede.'[1] Another section of his patrons belonged to commercial circles and were men who may have felt themselves cut off from much that would have been profitable to them through their inability to read classical or foreign languages. It was at the request of a mercer named William Prat that Caxton undertook the translation of *The Boke of Good Maners* (1487)

> to thende that it myght be had and vsed emonge the people for thamendement of their maners. and to thencreace of vertuous lyuying.[2]

He undertakes by his own judgment other translations such as *The Game and Playe of the Chesse* (second ed. 1483) which

> semed ful necessarye for to be had in englisshe / And in eschewyng of ydlenes And to thende that so*m*me which haue not seen it / ne v̄nderstonde frensshe ne latyn. I delybered in my self to translate it in to our maternal tonge. . . .[3]

As translator he has to make a critical selection of the work most valuable for translation. Because of his responsibility towards his audience matter has great importance in his eyes. He commends the study of the *Historie of Jason* (1477) to the Prince of Wales so that

> he may begynne to lerne rede Englissh. not for ony beaute or good Endyting of our englissh tonge that is therin. but for the nouelte of the histories whiche as I suppose hath not be had bifore the translacion herof. . . .[4],

Caxton, however, was by no means disposed to disregard quality of style in favour of gravity of matter. He notes stylistic qualities in his originals. The French source of his *Eneydos* pleased him

> by cause of the fayr and honest termes] wordes in frenshe / Whyche I neuer sawe to fore lyke, ne none so playsaunt ne so wel ordred. whiche booke as me semed sholde be moche requysyte to noble men to see as well for the eloquence as the historyes.[5]

[1] *Cordyale* (1479), Epilogue, *ibid.*, p. 39.
[2] Prologue, *ibid.*, p. 100.
[3] Prologue, *ibid.*, p. 12.
[4] Prologue, *ibid.*, p. 34.
[5] Prologue, *ibid.*, p. 107.

THE EARLIEST TUDOR PHASE

He is aware of the perennial translator's problem and works, he says:

> ... folowyng myn auctor as nygh as I can or may not chaungyng the sentence. ne // presumyng to adde ne mynusshe ony thing otherwyse than myne auctor hath made in Frensshe.[1]

He has advanced a long way towards a conception of translation as a literary activity with definite standards imposing certain obligations upon the translator. These obligations had been brought into prominence by the Wycliffite controversies, but Caxton is the earliest of the secular translators of this period to evolve such deliberate tenets. He is careful always, for the ultimate benefit of the English language and is eager to give it a grace and elegance similar to that of the French. When he has 'grete pleasyr and delyte...' in

> the fayr langage of frenshe whyche was in prose so well and compendiously sette and wreten,

he immediately decides that

> for so moche as this booke was newe and late maad and drawen in to frenshe / And neuer had seen hit in oure englisshe tonge / I thought in my self hit shold be a good besynes to translate hyt in to oure englissh....[2]

His position as critic and selector of language is all the more important because of his responsibility as printer, for he remembers

> that wordes ben perisshing vayne. and forgeteful / And writynges dwelle / and abyde permanent / ...[3]

A touchstone of literary and linguistic taste in this age is the attitude to Chaucer and the relative importance given to him as compared with Lydgate and Gower in the triad of poets to whom the Early Tudor writers looked for precedent and example. In an age which inclined to rank Lydgate highest as the master of elaborate expression, Caxton's independence of judgment is proved again by his discriminating praise of Chaucer. He speaks of the excellence of

---

[1] *The Historie of Jason* (1477), Prologue, *ibid.*, p. 33.
[2] *Le Recueil des Histoires de Troyes*, Prologue, *ibid.*, p. 4.
[3] *Mirrour of the World* (Second ed., 1490), Prologue, *ibid.*, p. 51.

EARLY TUDOR CRITICISM

Chaucer's style with a sincerity which makes his comment more than a conventional tribute. He appreciates the pressure behind Chaucer's work:

> For he wrytteth no voyde wordes / but alle hys mater is ful of hye and quycke sentence. . .[1]

and the fluent ease of his style seems to Caxton to mark an advance upon the earlier uncouthness of the language. He sees Chaucer as a benefactor of the English language, who

> by hys labour enbelysshyd / ornated / and made faire our englisshe / in thys Royame was had rude speche] Incongrue / as yet it appiereth by olde bookes / whyche at thys day ought not to haue place ne be compared emong ne to hys beauteuous volumes / and aournate writynges / . . . of many a noble historye as wel in metre as in ryme and prose / . . .[2]

In the more minute examination of the way in which Chaucer achieves this effect of polish and cogency Caxton reveals his own predilection for simplicity and sincerity, the qualities by which Chaucer

> comprehended hys maters in short / quyck and hye sentences / eschewyng prolyxyte / castyng away the chaf of superfluyte / and shewyng the pyked grayn of sentence / vtteryd by crafty and sugred eloquence /[3]

Caxton's comments on literature and language are so discriminating, his attitude to translation so thoughtful that they point to a mind alive to the many currents of thought in his age, a mind which deliberately selects and formulates its decision. He was no scholar and is therefore untouched by any intimation of the intellectual progress of the next phase of the Early Tudor period. There is in him a genuine manifestation of the critical spirit, independently developed and consistently sustained.

The same problems of style and diction which exercise the prose-writers Berners and Caxton occupy the attention of the poets of the period as deeply. There was in poetry the same opposition between the aureate language and the plain

---
[1] *The Book of Fame* (1483), Epilogue, *ibid.*, p. 69.
[2] *Canterbury Tales* (Second ed., 1484), Prohemye, *ibid.*, p. 90.
[3] *Ibid.*

THE EARLIEST TUDOR PHASE

style and the same dissatisfaction with the resources of English.

In the mediaeval tradition of allegory passed on to the Tudor period by Lydgate, the diction of poetry was removed as far as possible from the language of everyday life. It was governed by the elaborate rules of rhetoric and the term 'rethoryke,' with the adjectives 'facundious' (Berners) or 'golden' (Hawes), therefore becomes equated with ornate speech. 'Elocucyon' is defined by Hawes as the process of selecting as words suitable for poetry the less colloquial terms of the language. It carefully divides

> ... dulcet speche / frome the langage rude
> Tellynge the tale / in termes eloquent
> The barbary tongue / it doth ferre exclude
> Electynge wordes / whiche are expedyent
> In latyn / or in englysshe / after the entent
> Encensynge out / the aromatyke fume
> Our langage rude / to exyle and consume.[1]

This separation of poetry as fire and air from the baser earth of the language of ordinary usage resulted in a jargon considered purely poetic. The poet's isolated glory is described by Hawes in terms as 'refulgent' as his images:

> Carbuncles / in the most derke nyght
> Doth shyne fayre / with clere radyant beames
> Exylyng derkenes / with his rayes lyght
> And so these poetes / with theyr golden streames
> Deuoyde our rudenes / with grete fyry lemes
> Theyr centencyous verses / are refulgent
> Encensynge out / the odour redolent. ...[2]

He praises the achievement of Lydgate for his services to the English language. He says that his master has made

> ... our tongue / so clerely puryfyed
> That the vyle termes / shoulde nothynge arage
> As lyke a pye / to chattre in a cage
> But for to speke / with Rethoryke formally
> In the good ordre / withouten vylany.[3]

[1] Op. cit., p. 41, ll. 918–924. [2] Ibid., p. 48, ll. 1128–1134.
[3] Ibid., p. 49, ll. 1165–1169.

EARLY TUDOR CRITICISM

Wherever the Lydgatian tradition is continued into the Tudor period, the aureate language is its formal accompaniment linking England with the general taste for elaborate language in contemporary Europe. Hawes is no mean follower of his avowed master. Skelton in his allegorical work produces a vocabulary worthy of the loftiest aureate requirements. The opening of the *Garlande of Laurell* is typical of this vein, in its matter, the astronomical details and its hybrid, inkhorn language:

> Arectyng my syght towarde the zodyake,
> The sygnes xii for to beholde a farre,
> When Mars retrogradant reuersyd his bak,
> Lorde of the yere in his orbicular,
> Put vp his sworde, for he cowde make no warre,
> And whan Lucina plenarly did shyne,
> Scorpione ascendynge degrees twyse nyne. . . .[1]

Such rhetoric is not Skelton's natural language. He tends to the plain style, pungent in his satires, lighter and even graceful in some of his slighter lyrics such as those included in the *Garlande of Laurell*:

> Enuuwyd your colowre
> Is lyke the dasy flowre
> After the Aprill showre . . .[2]

and

> mirry Margarete
> As mydsomer flowre,
> Ientyll as fawcoun
> Or hawke of the towre,[3]

and the opening of the lyric *To maystres Isabell Pennell* quoted above:

> By saynt Mary, my lady,
> Your mammy and your dady
> Brought forth a godely babi.[4]

Yet Skelton seems to feel that English is clumsy for poetical purposes, unsuitable for an ornate style and not yet

[1] *Ibid.*, Vol. I, p. 361, ll. 1-7. [2] *Ibid.*, Vol. I, p. 401, ll. 985-986.
Ibid., pp. 401-402, ll. 1004-1007. [4] *Ibid.*, Vol. I, p. 400, ll. 973-975.

16

THE EARLIEST TUDOR PHASE

capable of ease and simplicity. He seizes eagerly upon the stock complaint of its 'rudeness':

> Our naturall tong is rude,
> And hard to be enneude
> With pullysshed termes lusty;
> Our language is so rusty
> So cankered, and so full
> Of frowardes, and so dull,
> That if I wolde apply
> To wryte ornatly,
> I wot not where to fynd
> Termes to serue my mynde,[1]

Yet he does not, like Hawes, believe it completely inferior to Latin. His use of English for so many purposes indicates that he has some hope of its future possibilities, whereas Hawes deplores its unfitness for any serious literary purpose. He feels it a thankless task to try to explain the intricacies of astronomy, for instance, in English:

> What sholde I wryte more in this mater hye
> In my maternall tonge opprest with ignoraunce
> For who that lyst to lerne astronomye
> He shall fynde all fruytfull pleasaunce
> In the latyn tongue by goodly ordenaunce.[2]

Skelton feels some apology necessary for submitting a work in English to men accustomed to Latin as the language of literature. Yet in spite of his diffidence, his apology has a tone hopeful of the reception which will be accorded to it. In 'Lenuoy' of the *Garlande of Laurell* he defends his use of English thus:

> Go, litill quaire,
> Demene you faire;
> Take no dispare,
> Though I you wrate
> After this rate
> In Englysshe letter;
> So moche the better

[1] *Phyllyp Sparowe*, Ibid., Vol. I, pp. 74-75, ll. 774-783.
[2] *Op. cit.*, p. 112, ll. 2906-2910.

EARLY TUDOR CRITICISM

> Welcome shall ye
> To sum men be:
> For Latin warkis
> Be good for clerkis;
> Yet now and then
> Sum Latin men
> May happely loke
> Vpon your boke.[1]

His gift of forcible expression is, indeed, in flat contradiction to conventional deprecation and the alleged 'poverty' of English. It is a stern contrast with the diaphanous tissue of words spun by mediaeval allegorists. Truly Skeltonic in spirit is the assertion in the verses *Howe the Douty Duke of Albany, etc:*

> What though my stile be rude?
> With trouthe it is ennewde;
> Trouth ought to be rescude,
> Trouthe should nat be subdude.[2]

and in the same work:

> Though your Englishe be rude,
>   Barreyne of eloquence,
> Yet, breuely to conclude,
>   Grounded is your sentence
> On trouthe, vnder defence
> Of all trewe Englyshemen,
> This mater to credence
> That I wrate with my pen.[3]

Just as *Colyn Cloute* marks the severance from the allegorical in favour of the dramatic, so the clipped, sharp style marks the emancipation from rhetoric and is commented on by Colyn for its lack of grace redeemed by pungency:

> For though my ryme be ragged,
> Tattered and iagged,
> Rudely rayne beaten,
> Rusty and moughte eaten,
> If ye take well therwith,
> It hath in it some pyth.[4]

[1] *Op. cit.*, Vol. I, p. 422, ll. 1533–1547. [2] *Ibid.*, Vol. II, p. 80, ll. 419–422.
[3] *Ibid.*, p. 83, ll. 516–523. [4] *Ibid.*, Vol. I, p. 313, ll. 53–58.

THE EARLIEST TUDOR PHASE

Skelton's preference for plain and direct expression is evident in his praise of Chaucer as in Caxton's. Chaucer's matter he finds

> delectable
> Solacious and commendable;
> His Englysh well alowed,
> So as it is enprowed. ....[1]
> His termes were not darke,
> But plesaunt, easy, and playne;
> No worde he wrote in vayne. ....[2]

He concedes the fact that Lydgate

> Wryteth after an hyer rate;
> It is dyffuse to fynde
> The sentence of his mynde. ....[3]

From a comparison of his comments it would seem that there was during his day a desire to find a middle style between that of Chaucer, for

> ... men wold haue amended
> His Englysh, whereat they barke,
> And mar all they warke,[4]

and that of Lydgate, for

> some men fynde a faute,
> And say he wryteth to haute. ....[5]

Chaucer and Lydgate mark the limits within which the compromise of style must be made. The setting up of these standards and the conscious comparison made indicate the working of a critical spirit. The same dissatisfaction is felt by the verse translators as by Skelton coercing his thought into English. These experience especial difficulties in making some approximation between the original language and English since a completely literal rendering is less suitable or possible for poetry than for prose. Hence, poetic renderings from other languages are, particularly in this early period, adaptations rather than translations and the translators have a less complete sense of responsibility than those

[1] *Ibid.*, p. 75, ll. 790-793. [2] *Ibid.*, ll. 801-803. [3] *Ibid.*, ll. 804-807.
[4] *Ibid.*, ll. 797-799. [5] *Ibid.*, ll. 811-812.

EARLY TUDOR CRITICISM

who worked in prose. Their conscience is not entirely asleep, however, and in Gavin Douglas' comments on his method of translating there is some realization that divergence from the original must not be carried too far. He is willing to try to preserve the meaning in order that his version may show

> Na thyng alterit in substance the sentence,
> Thocht scant perfyte observit bene eloquens.[1]

He accuses Caxton, on this score, of such alteration that the translation and the original were 'na mair like than the devill and Sanct Austyne.'[2] He makes a critical distinction between the translating activity and the creative.

> Traist wele, to follow ane fixt sentence or mater,
> Is mair practik, difficill, and mair strater,
> Thocht thyne engyne be elevait and hie,
> Than for to write all ways at libertie.[3]

The choice of an original implies, of course, an opinion of its value. Douglas appreciates the excellence of Virgil:

> I haue translait a volum wondirfull.
> So profund was this wark at I haue said,
> Me semyt oft throw the deip sey to waid,
> And sa mysty vmquhyle this poesy,
> My spreit was reft half deill in extasy.[4]

He has chosen the very fountain-head of eloquence:

> ... I haue not interpryt ne translate
> Every burell rude poet divulgait,
> Na meyn endyte, nor empty wordis vayn,
> Commone engyne, nor style barbarian;
> Bot in that art of eloquens the fluide
> Maiste cheif, profund and copyus plenitude.[5]

His appreciation of Virgil's style makes him aware of the discrepancy between the limpid Latin and the halting

---

[1] *Poetical Works*, ed. J. Small (1874), Vol. 4, p. 227. All further references will be to this edition.
[2] *Ibid.*, Vol. 2, p. 7.   [3] *Ibid.*, p. 12, ll. 15–18.
[4] *Ibid.*, Vol. 4, p. 227, ll. 15–18.   [5] *Ibid.*, p. 225, ll. 27–32.

THE EARLIEST TUDOR PHASE

uncouthness of the vernacular. For his eulogy of Virgil he uses the customary hyperbole and ornate speech enjoined upon him by fashion, praising Virgil as

> Gemme of ingine and fluide of eloquence,
> Thou peirles perle, patroun of poetrie,
> Rois, register, palme, laurer and glory,
> Chosin cherbukle, cheif flour and cedir tree....[1]

For the actual translation he refuses to attempt to reproduce the qualities of such a poet, incompatible with the unpolished vernacular,

> Kepand na facund rethorik castis fair,
> Bot haymly plane termes famyliar.[2]

He decides that the plain style and a free translation of the Latin to preserve the meaning as closely as possible will best serve the purposes of his work.

> Besyde Latyne our langage is imperfite,
> Quhilk in sum part is the caus and the wite,
> Quhy that of Virgillis vers the ornate bewtie
> Intill our toung may nocht obseruit be.[3]

Illustrations of words which cannot be expressed in English with the Latin's precise distinctions support his argument. The use of the plain style is justified by the consequent appeal to a wider audience including the unlearned. The work must sustain the criticisms of the scholarly, who are familiar with the original, but the main object is to reproduce a great work as simply as possible for the profit and pleasure of those who will read it for its own intrinsic value. It will

> ... to onletterit folk be red on hycht,
> That erst was bot with clerkis comprehend.[4]

The atmosphere of change and controversy reflected in the prose, poetry and translation of the late fifteenth and early sixteenth century, the discussion of style and diction, the evidence of fashions in language, the disuse of old forms or their modification for new purposes—all these trends

---

[1] *Ibid.*, Vol. 2, p. 3, ll. 4–7. [2] *Ibid.*, Vol. 4, p. 227, ll. 5–6.
[3] *Ibid.*, Vol. 2, p. 14, ll. 27–30. [4] *Ibid.*, Vol. 4, p. 230, ll. 26–27.

EARLY TUDOR CRITICISM

show that it was a time for the consideration of decisions literary and linguistic. The writers of this period dissociate themselves sufficiently from the pressure of creation to take stock of their position, to consider the achievement of their forerunners and discuss the transmission of their models into the Tudor period. They are most preoccupied by the problems of the language which must be their instrument. It is compared and contrasted with foreign and classical languages, and conclusions are drawn which are important as foreshadowings of all the linguistic controversy of the later Tudor period. The stock complaints of uncouthness become more independent decisions.

No definite critical tenets can be deduced from this period. Its importance lies in the growth of a critical attitude rather than in the formulation of rules. It marks a new explicit attention to form and attempts to select from other literature whatever may promote English achievement. As a period highly sensitive to issues literary and linguistic, one of increasing vitality and promise, it may be regarded as an important prelude to the Tudor theme.

CHAPTER II

THE TRANSLATION OF THE BIBLE

SINCE the foundation upon which the Christian religion rests is a text, it is obvious that from the controversy concerning the propriety, aims and methods of Bible translation should issue some contribution to the study of the language and to the problem of translation which constitutes an important focus of critical discussion. The main issues are theological, but the men opposed to the translation of the Bible raise so many linguistic points to support their objections that attention is focussed upon language and upon the adequacy of English speech for the most onerous and exacting of all translations. Bible translators had to marshal their arguments in corresponding detail to defend their activity.

There has always been an incontrovertible use for the vernacular in religious instruction. Devotional and hortatory matter must be passed on to the layman in his own language and the instructor must have some access to this vernacular matter since so much depends upon citations of the Scriptures. All religious instructors were by no means learned themselves and therefore felt the need, as much as did their flock, of a standard source of reference. There was a strong conviction that it was

> spedful not oonly to the lewed peple but also to the lewed curatis to have bookis in Englisch of needful loore to the lewed peple; for many curatis kunnen not construe ne expoune her pater noster, ne aue, ne crede, ne the ten commaundementis, ne the seuene dedely synnes, ne many othere thingis, that thei ben bounden to knowe and to teche othere, as the lawe shewith.[1]

[1] Wycliffite tract belonging to the University of Cambridge. Author(s) unknown. See *The Holy Bible, containing the Old and New Testaments, with the Apocryphal Books, in the Earliest English Versions made from the Latin Vulgate by John Wycliffe and his Followers*, ed. J. Forshall and F. Madden (1850), Vol. I, p. xiv, note k.

Preaching, too, helped to maintain the continuity of the vernacular for devotional purposes. Reginald Pecock, a fearless advocate of 'reding . . in þe englisch bible,'[1] was quick to see the coincidence between oral instruction and reading in the vernacular, and

> for like causis for whiche clerkis prechen þe maters of þese seid bookis to þe peple in her comoun langage. . . .[2]

he writes his own books of instruction. He is convinced that there can be no harm in

> prentyng into hem abiding deuocioun, wiþoute þat þe peple haue at hem silf in writing which þei mowe ofte rede or heere oft rad þe substancial poyntis and trouþis whiche ben to hem to be prechid bi mouþe.[3]

From the latter half of the fourteenth century onwards the use of vernacular versions of the Bible had been hotly debated. Opposition to the plan of making the text of the Bible available to the layman was based upon the belief that scriptural interpretation was the prerogative of the Church alone. This interpretation was fourfold.[4] Holy Writ was to be expounded by the clergy

> sometimes morally, sometimes allegorically, and sometimes anagogically, and not according to the literal meaning of the words, as in the biblical poems, which in no case are to be interpreted as literally true.[5]

The use of a Lollard text of the Bible, unglossed, was held to be excessively harmful, as it was based upon the literal interpretation only. This was the orthodox and most serious accusation against the Lollards. By reason of the stress laid upon the text of the Bible, a spate of discussion

---

[1] *Donet* (after 1443), ed. Miss E. V. Hitchcock, E.E.T.S. (Original Series 156), 1921, p. 172, l. 2.
[2] *The Reule of Crysten Religion*, ed. W. C. Greet, E.E.T.S. (Original Series 171), 1927. Prologue, p. 197, b.
[3] *Ibid.*, p. 20.
[4] Cf. H. Caplan, 'The Four Senses of Scriptural Interpretation and the Mediaeval Theory of Preaching,' *Speculum*, 4 (1929).
[5] From the translation of a tract in defence of Nicholas Hereford by Thomas Palmer, against a tract by the Lollard Walter Boute tried for heresy, 1393. See M. Deanesly, *The Lollard Bible* (1920), Ch. II, p. 288.

THE TRANSLATION OF THE BIBLE

concerning the character and capabilities of the English language ensues. This need not imply an increased linguistic consciousness. It is more probable that the recurrent assertion of the inadequacy of English was an easy argument for anyone who objected on any grounds to the translation of the Bible. The issues of this controversy were theological, but the method led to linguistic criticism as a by-product.

Before the time of Wycliffe there had appeared no authorized complete version of the Scriptures in English. Portions had been translated by Caedmon, King Alfred and others in the Anglo-Saxon period and the Wycliffites quoted these early attempts as a justification of their own.[1] The opposition of the Church in the fourteenth century was not expressed in any definite mandate, but was tacitly understood. The appearance (1380–1383) of the versions associated with the name of Wycliffe organized the Church's defences. Vigorous debates ensued, in which the moving spirit was John Purvey.[2] At Oxford in particular, battle raged between friars and Lollards. The former set their faces firmly against translation of the Bible in general and into English in particular. The arguments of the master of the Franciscans at Oxford, William Butler[3] and the friar Thomas Palmer[4] are typical of the Church's general attitude to Bible translations. The assertion of the inevitable inaccuracy of an English translation is persistently advanced[5] and appears in official

---

[1] Cf. Purvey, Prologue to 'alle the bokis of the Bible of the oolde testament' (c.1388) 'Lord God! sithen at the bigynnyng of feith so manie men translatiden into Latyn, and to greet profyt of Latyn men, lat oo symple creature of God translate into English, for profyt of English men; for if worldli clerkis loken wel here croniclis and bokis, thei shulden fynde, that Bede translatide the bible, and expounide myche in Saxon, that was English, either comoun langage of this lond, in his tyme; and not oneli Bede, but also king Alured, that foundide Oxenford, translatide in his laste daies the bigynning of the Sauter into Saxon, and wolde more, if he hadde lyued lengere.' (Forshall and Madden, *op. cit.*, Vol. I, p. 59.)
[2] See M. Deanesly, *op. cit.*, Ch. II, pp. 268–297.
[3] *Ibid.*, p. 289.
[4] *Ibid.*, p. 290.
[5] William Butler, *contra translationem Anglicanam* (fol. 202, col. 1). 'Sic constat quod libri si multiplicarentur essent mendosi, qui cito legentes inducerent ad errorem: ergo, periculosum esset tales libros scribere.' (See M. Deanesly, *op. cit.*, Appendix 2, p. 401.) Thomas Palmer, *De translatione reverse scripturae in linguam Anglicanam.* '(Ad quintum) nego consequentiam, quia in linguam Hebraicam,

EARLY TUDOR CRITICISM

form in the prohibition of the use of vernacular translations by the provincial council of Oxford in 1408[1]:

> Also, since it is dangerous, as S. Jerome witnesses, to translate the text of holy scripture from one language into another, because in such translations the same meaning is not easily retained in all particulars: . . . therefore we decree and ordain that no-one shall in future translate on his own authority any text of holy scripture into the English tongue or into any other tongue, by way of book, booklet or treatise. Nor shall any man read this kind of book, booklet or treatise.[2]

This decree marks the end of one phase of the argument. The nature of the battle was determined and it was obvious that much of the struggle would be played out on linguistic grounds. Both sides focussed their attention on the methods and exactitudes of translation and the English language had become a weapon for both the one to attack with a charge of heresy through mistranslation, construed as wilful, the other to defend by unassailable excellence, achieved by careful study of a translator's duty.

The prohibition of the use of vernacular versions proved quite ineffectual. Large numbers of texts were in circulation, such as those seen by Sir Thomas More.[3] Men of the persuasion of Wycliffe were strongly convinced that

> the gospelle is rewle, be the whilk ich cristen man owes to lyf.[4]

The demand for general reading of the Bible was great enough to ensure a wide circulation of English texts for

---

Graecam et Latinam ipsa potest transferri, non tamen sic potest in omnem linguam, quia alphabeto Latinorum non utuntur neque Graecorum neque Hebraicorum, et licet uterentur illo non tamen expediret neque deberet omnia in illa transferri, propter quaedam ante dicta.' (See M. Deanesly, *op. cit.*, p. 435.)

[1] See D. Wilkins, *Concilia Magnae Britanniae et Hiberniae* . . . (1737), Vol. 3, p. 317.
[2] See M. Deanesly, *op. cit.*, p. 296.
[3] '. . . my self haue seen and can shew you bybles fayre and old writen in englishe whiche haue been knowen [and] seen by the byshop of the dyoces, [and] left in leye mens handes [and] womens to suche as he knewe for good and catholike folk . . .' *Dialogue concernynge heresyes* (1528). See *English Works of Sir Thomas More*, ed. W. E. Campbell (1931), Vol. 2, f. 234.
See M. Deanesly, *op. cit.*, Ch. I, pp. 3–14, for discussion of the identity of these Bibles.
[4] Quoted by Forshall and Madden, *op. cit.*, p. x, note f.

many lewd men are, that gladly wold kon the gospelle if it were draghen in to Englisch tung, and so it suld do grete profete to man saule. . . .[1]

A written version would stabilize for men in general the necessary sources of knowledge and lead to closer study. Its advocates assert

> that it is leefful and spedful to hem that kunne rede, and name-liche to gentellis, to haue Goddis lawe writen in bookis, that thei mowen red it, and so the better kunne; for it is a comoun sawe, and soth it is, Worde and wynd and mannes mynde is ful schort, but letter writen dwellith.[2]

An outcome of this would be the fixing of a standard language, the choice of diction and style which would be acceptable to the learned and comprehensible to the layman, the same two-fold demand which was recognized by the secular translators. Such a combination was even more imperative to Bible translators than to them, because of the supreme importance of a text which extended beyond scholarship to salvation.

With the Reformation came a renewed assertion of the right of the individual to interpret the Scriptures for himself and a rejection of the authority of the Church as the source of inspired interpretation. Men such as Thomas More realized the danger of this uncontrolled individualism and the errors to which it might lead. In his *Dialogue concernynge heresyes*,[3] meeting the arguments of the Messenger step by step, he gives a comprehensive survey of the relations of the Church and the Reformers at this time. Discussion of the use of vernacular Bibles takes an important place in the argument, since the Church feared so deeply the effect this might have upon her prerogative. The essential point which More enforces is that the prohibition of vernacular versions is not directed against translation *per se*, but against inaccurate and therefore dangerous versions tending to the fostering of heresy. The author answers the Messenger's challenge:

[1] *Ibid.*   [2] *Ibid.*, p. xiv, note k.   [3] *Op. cit.*, Vol. 2.

EARLY TUDOR CRITICISM

> I see no cause why the cleargie shoulde kepe the byble out of ley mennes handes, that can no more but theyr mother tong,[1]

by a modified view of the prohibition :

> ... I haue shewed you y^t they kepe none frō thē, but such translacion as be either not yet approued for good, or such as be alredi reproued for naught, as Wikliffes was & Tindals.[2]

The Messenger insists that the attitude of the clergy is in the main much less liberal:

> I heare in euerye place almost where I find any learned man of thē, their mindes all set theron to kepe ye scripture frō vs. And they seke out for that parte euery rotten reason that they can find, & set them forth solenely to the shew, though fyue of those reasons bee not woorth a figge.[3]

Among these reasons he cites the recurrent excuse of the crudity and inadequacy of the English language:

> Yet they say further y^t it is hard to trās-late ye scripture out of one tong into an other, and specially they say into ours, which they call a tong vulgare & barba-rous.[4]

Thomas More in answer delivers the famous eulogy of the possibilities of the English language which sets the seal of scholarly approval upon the use of the vernacular in the sixteenth century. It is all the more notable by reason of its early date, before the work of the secular translators and the convictions of scholars such as Cheke and the Cambridge circle could prove its justice. More refutes the accusation of 'barbarous', which was levelled too glibly against the vernaculars by men of an age intoxicated with the study of Greek and Latin excellence:

> For as for that our tong is called barbarous, is but a fantasye. For so is, as euery lerned mā knoweth, euery straunge language to other And if they would call it barayn of wordes, there is no doubt but it is plenteous enough to expresse our myndes in anye thing whereof one mā hath vsed to speke with another.[5]

He finds the difficulties of translation no greater for the English language than for any other and appreciates the

[1] *Op. cit.*, Vol. 2, f. 240.   [2] *Ibid.*, f. 241.   [3] *Ibid.*   [4] *Ibid.*   [5] *Ibid.*, f. 243.

THE TRANSLATION OF THE BIBLE

discipline of reproducing the original as exactly as possible. The opinion that this is impossible is no more valid for the work of the sixteenth century than for that of any other age when translation was attempted:

> Nowe as touchynge the / difficultie which a translatour fyndeth in expressing well and liuely the sentēce of his author, whiche is hard alwaye to do so surely but that he shall sometime minyshe eyther of the sentence or of the grace that it bereth in the formar tong: that poynt hath lyen in their lyght that haue translated the scrypture alreadye eyther out of greke into latine, or out of hebrue into any of them both, as by many translaciōs which we rede already, to them that be learned appereth.[1]

The convictions of Erasmus, More and More's antagonist, Tyndale, are essentially the same. Erasmus' expression of belief in the usefulness of a translation for general use is the most eloquent of them all:

> And truely do I dissent from those men / whiche wold not that the scripture of Christ shuld be trāslated in to all tonges / that it might be reade diligently of the private and seculare men and women / ...
>
> I wold to god / yᵉ ploumā wold singe a texte of the scripture at his plowbeme / And that the wever at his lowme / with this wold driue away the tediousnes of tyme. I wold the wayfaringe man with this pastyme / wold expelle the werynes of his iorney.[2]

Erasmus' publication in 1516 of the Greek text of the New Testament, accompanied by a new Latin translation,[3] marks the scholarly approach to the problem of translation and recognizes the importance of securing an exact and accurate text of the original before further translations could be attempted.

Tyndale was as zealous as Erasmus for the enlightenment of the unlearned people, having

> perceaved by experyence, how that it was impossible to stablysh

---

[1] *Ibid.*, f. 243–f. 244.
[2] Prefixed to his Greek translation of the New Testament, translated by William Roye (printed at Antwerp 1529).
[3] Revised editions issued 1519, 1522.

29

EARLY TUDOR CRITICISM

the laye people in any truth, excepte the scripture were playnly layde before their eyes in their mother tonge, that they might se the processe, ordre and meaninge of the texte.[1]

Upon the principle Erasmus, More and Tyndale are agreed. The emphasis of the prolonged controversy concerning the use of vernacular versions has shifted. It is no longer confined to the issue between the Church, unwilling to yield its prestige as guardian of Scriptural mysteries, and the translators, eager to make them available to all. The controversies of the Early Tudor period are more purely linguistic, debating more subtle points of diction and translation with all the sharpened critical faculty which is a product of so many other controversies of this age.

Tyndale comments upon the carping spirit in which translations of the Scriptures were examined:

> For they which in tymes paste were wonte to loke on no more scripture than they founde in their duns or soch like develysh doctryne, haue yet now so narowlye loked on my translatyon, that there is not so much as one I therin if it lacke a tytle over his hed, but they haue noted it, and nombre it vnto the ignorant people for an heresy.[2]

He was sure of the fitness of the English language for his high purposes and refuted the imputation of its uncouthness as vehemently as Sir Thomas More, citing like him the tradition behind his work:

> Saynt Hierom also trāslated the bible in to his mother tonge. Why maye not we also? They wil saye it can not be translated in to oure tonge it is so rude. It is not so rude as they ar false lyers.[3]

Although so closely allied in theory, they were bitterly opposed on the detail of the practice. Tyndale had examined and compared the qualities of Latin, Greek, Hebrew and English, so that his translation is undertaken with the full

---
[1] Preface to Genesis in his version of the Pentateuch, printed 1530. Quoted A. W. Pollard, *Records of the English Bible* (1911), p. 95.
For account of the Pentateuch, see E. Gordon Duff, *A Short Account of Tindale's Pentateuch* (1910).
[2] *Ibid.* See Pollard, *op. cit.*, p. 94.
[3] *The obediēce of a Christen Man* (1528), fol. xv[v].

30

THE TRANSLATION OF THE BIBLE

sense of the essential character of each language upon which the theory of translation lays such stress. He decides that

> ... the greke tonge agreeth moare with the english then with the latyne. And the propirties of the hebrue tonge agreth a thousande tymes moare with the english then with the latyne. The maner of speakynge is both one so that in a thousande places thou neadest not but to trāslate it into the english worde for worde, whē thou must seke a compasse in the latyne and yet shalt have moch worke to trāslate it welfaveredly / so that it have the same grace ād swetnesse / sence and pure vnderstandinge with it in the latyne / as it hath in the hebrue. . . .[1]

Nevertheless, one of More's accusations against Tyndale is that he has ignored the authority of the vernacular and has

> mysse translated three woordes of great weighte and euerye one of them is as I suppose more than thryse three tymes repeted and rehearsed in the booke. . . . The one is . . . this worde (priestes). The other the Churche. The thyrde Charitye. . . .[2]

Tyndale had translated these words respectively as 'seniors', 'congregation,' and 'love,' and More says:

> Nowe dooe these names in our English toungue, / neyther expresse the thynges that be mēt by them,[3]

this reason preceding the theological objection that

> he had a mischieuous minde in the chaunge.[4]

The heretical construction which More elaborates upon the evidence of these words is significant of the grave importance attached to the choice of words with accepted meanings which would offend no conscience. Like the secular translator, Tyndale had to observe the rules of usage established in the language of everyday speech. More amplifies his statement and reiterates what is one of the most important principles of linguistic criticism in the Early Tudor period. Continuing his argument concerning the application of the word 'congregation' as against the word 'church,' he says:

[1] *Ibid.*
[2] *Dialogue concernynge heresyes, op. cit.*, f. 220.
[3] *Ibid.*, ff. 220-221.
[4] *Ibid.*, f. 221.

31

And I sayed and yet I say, that this is trew of ye vsuall sygnificacyon of these wordes them selfe in the englyshe tonge, by the comē custume of vs englyshe peple, that eyther now do vse these wordes in our langage, or that haue vsed byfore oure dayes. And I saye that this comen custume and vsage of speche is the onely thynge, by whyche we knowe the ryght and proper sygnifycacyon of any worde / in so mych that yf a worde were taken oute of laten, french, or spaynishe, [and] were for lakke of vnderstandynge of the tonge from whense yt came, vsed for a nother thynge in englyshe then yt was in the formare tonge: then sygnyfyeth it in england none other thyng than as we vse yt and vnderstande therby, what so euer yt sygnifye anywhere elles.[1]

This is a concise formulation of the great principle of 'custom' or 'use' which was to emerge later in the century in the discussions of progressive critics. The very augmenting of the English language by borrowings from foreign languages, to be hotly debated in the 'ink-horn' controversy, was a particularly urgent problem for the translator. Being forced sometimes to coin equivalents in English of words in his text, he, almost more than original writers, had to set himself some principle to control this tendency. More clearly apprehends the moderation and care for the character of the language which alone could make foreign coinages valuable additions to the language. Careful scrutiny of every word is an essential part of the translator's task. More rejects Tyndale's attempts to justify his choice of renderings because he cannot

> saye that thys is the proper sygnyfycacyon of that worde, [church] whyche is the thynge that a translatour must regarde.[2]

Even if Tyndale's religious persuasions cannot be reconciled with his own, More demands at least the use of accurate English in his translations:

> ... though I can not make hym by no meane to wryte trewe mater, I wolde haue hym yet at the leste wyse wryte trewe englyshe.[3]

---

[1] *The Cōfutacyon of Tyndale's answere, made by syr Thomas More knyght lorde chaūcellor of Englonde*, sig. p. iii{v}.   [2] *Ibid.*, fol. cxix.   [3] *Ibid.*, fol. clxxxi.

THE TRANSLATION OF THE BIBLE

A general preoccupation with the English language, evolving a considerable body of critical comment and *dicta*, therefore plays an important part in one of the most serious controversies in the Early Tudor period. Many of the pronouncements thrown off in the heat of argument contribute to the gradual building up of a critical tradition. These are particularly valuable when they throw light upon the personalities who were the moving spirits of the age, but who yet remain elusive, their work being no adequate indication of their personal influence. Sir John Cheke, the acknowledged intellectual leader of his time, takes his place in the controversy concerning Bible translation and another fragment can be added to the mosaic which makes up his portrait.

The same names recur as leaders either of liberal thought or obscurantism, whether in a religious or secular context. Cheke and Stephen Gardiner, Bishop of Winchester, soon to be engaged in a fierce struggle about the reformed pronunciation of Greek, pursue their respective courses in a controversy concerning the language of Bible translation.

Gardiner strenuously opposed the printing of the Great Bible in 1539. When Grafton and Whitchurch collected from Paris the material left after the English printers there had fled, accused of heresy, they tried to continue their work in England. This they did

> not without great trouble and losse, for the hatred of the bishops namely, Steuen Gardiner and his fellowes, who mightily did stomacke and maligne the printing thereof.[1]

Gardiner had already in 1535 taken some part in the projected 'Bishops' Bible.' Cromwell delegated to each Bishop a portion of the New Testament for his correction and Gardiner seems to have completed his share, for he speaks in a letter to Cromwell of June 10th, 1535, of

> having finished the translation of Saynt Luke and Saynt John, wherin I have spent a gret labour.[2]

[1] Fox, *Actes and Monumentes* (4th ed., 1583), p. 1191. (Quoted A. W. Pollard, *op. cit.*, p. 227.)
[2] See *State Papers of Henry VIII*, Vol. 1, p. 430. 'From Crumwell's Correspondence in the Chapter House, Bundle W.' (Quoted A. W. Pollard, *op. cit.*, pp. 196–197, note 2.)

EARLY TUDOR CRITICISM

He appears again in the condemnation of the Great Bible at a Convocation in 1542, at which this version was voted unfit for use

> nisi prius debite castigetur et examinetur juxta eam Bibliam, quae communiter in ecclesia Anglicana legitur.[1]

Again the focus of the dispute is linguistic. Gardiner, ever zealous for the cause of the Latin language and unwilling to sacrifice the Latin element in the vernacular, drew up a list of about a hundred words which he proposed should be retained

> pro eorum germano et nativo intellectu et rei majestate, quoad poterit vel in sua natura retineri, vel quam accommodatissime fieri possit in Anglicum sermonem verti.[2]

Had the future of English Bible translation lain in the hands of men of Gardiner's persuasion, the compromise between dignity and simplicity would not have been accomplished so successfully as it was established in the work of Tyndale and confirmed by Miles Coverdale.

Cheke, as anxious to preserve the Saxon character of English as Gardiner was to obscure it with Latin, issued a counterblast to the Latinists in his translation of the Gospel of St. Matthew from the original Greek into Saxon speech. He substituted native formations even for the Latin derivatives tactfully used by Tyndale. A comparison with other versions[3] shows that Cheke's alterations did not receive the

---

[1] See Wilkins' *Concilia*, Vol. 31, pp. 860 *seq.* (Quoted A. W. Pollard, *op. cit.*, p. 272.)

[2] See Wilkins' *Concilia*, Vol. 3, pp. 860 *seq.* (Quoted A. W. Pollard, *op. cit.*, p. 273.)

[3] Comparative table of equivalents in the versions of Cheke and others. (Quoted from edition by James Goodwin, 1843, Introd., p. 18.)

Cheke			Wyclif. 1380	Tyndale. 1534	Authorized Version. 1611
outpeopling.	I.	17.	transmygracioun.	captivite.	carrying away.
wiseards.	II.	16.	astromyens.	wyse men.	wise men.
moond.	IV.	24.	lunatik.	lunatyke.	lunaticke.
tollers.	V.	46.	pupplicans.	publicans.	publicans.
groundwrought.	VII.	25.	foundid.	grounded.	founded.
hunderder.	VIII.	5.	centurien.	centurion.	centurion.
frosent.	Note X.		apostlis.	apostles.	apostles.
biwordes.	XIII.	3.	parablis.	similitudes.	parables.
orders.	XV.	2.	tradiciouns.	tradicions.	tradition.
freschman.	XXIII.	15.	prosilite.	[circumlocution].	proselyte.
crossed.	XXVII.	22.	crucified.	crucified.	crucified.

THE TRANSLATION OF THE BIBLE

sanction of later versions. They merely prove that the best course for the English language was the judicious admixture of other elements advocated by men such as Sir Thomas Wilson and Sir Thomas Elyot. The type of Germanic compound which he tried to revive had been largely given up. Cheke's aim was to construct a vocabulary which would be comprehensible to all who knew only their native language, but the words he proposed to substitute for familiar foreign compounds were as alien to such people as Gardiner's vocabulary would have been. It proves the pervasive interest in language in the sixteenth century to find in the theological field the same conflicting principles as in other scholarly discussions.

The stormy progress of the translation of the Bible into English leaves in its wake a trail of comment upon the exigencies of the labour. This demanded the co-operation of the learned with single-minded men who had not their 'wit ocupied about worldli thingis'.[1] The Lollard Bible was produced with a great deal of labour:

> First, this symple creature hadde myche trauaile, with diuerse felawis and helperis, to gedere manie elde biblis and othere doctouris, and comune glosis, and to make oo Latyn bible sumdel trewe; and thanne to studie it of the newe, the texte with the glose, and othere doctouris, as he miʒte gete, and speciali Lire on the elde testament, that helpide ful myche in this werk; the thridde tyme to counseile with elde gramariens, and elde dyuynis, of . . . harde sentencis, hou tho miʒten best be vndurstonden and translatid; the iiij. tyme to translate as cleerli as he coude to the sentence, and to haue manie gode felawis and kunnynge at the correcting of the translacioun.[2]

In the Early Tudor period, when translation had become the pastime of learned men and of the cultured aristocracy, Bible translation was still this all-absorbing discipline. Nicholas Udall recognizes the exacting nature of the Bible translator's duty, that

> . . . the thing is suche as muste so throughlye occupie and

[1] Purvey's Prologue. (Forshall and Madden, *op. cit.*, Vol. 1, Preface, p. 60.)
[2] *Ibid.*, p. 57.

possesse the dooer, and must haue hym so attente to applie that same exercise onely, that he may not duryng that season take in hande any other trade of buisinesse whereby to purchase his lyuing: besides that the thing cannot bee dooen without bestowyng of long tyme, greate watchyng, muche peines, diligente studye....[1]

He reiterates Gavin Douglas' distinction between the freedom of the creative activity and the watchfully critical process of translation. He explains that

the laboure selfe is of it selfe a more peinefull and a more tedious thyng, then for a manne to write or prosecute anye argumente of hys owne inuencion. A manne hath his owne inuencion readye at his own pleasure without lettes or stoppes to make suche discourse as his argumente requireth: but a translatour muste of force in manier at euerye other woorde staigh, and suspende bothe his cogitacion and his penne to looke vpon his autoure, so that he mighte in equall tyme make thrise so muche, as he can bee hable to translate.[2]

This is a clear recognition of the unremitting exercise of judgment called for in translation, the double demands of the original and the rendering and the responsibility imposed upon the translator to make this rendering as exact as is consonant with the terms of his own language of translation.

This responsibility enforces a close study of the methods by which the meaning may be transmitted unchanged into another idiom. The conclusion of the Bible translators is that the literal equivalents of words in both languages must be sacrificed if necessary to keep *sententia* unimpaired. They know that

a translatour hath greet nede to studie wel the sentence, both bifore and aftir, and loke that suche equiuok wordis acorde with the sentence....[3]

The Wycliffites found at an earlier date that the best translation from Latin into English is

---

[1] Translation of *The Paraphrases of Erasmus vpon the newe testament* (1551). The Preface 'Unto the Kinges Maiestie.'
[2] *Ibid.*
[3] Purvey's Prologue. (Forshall and Madden, *op. cit.*, Preface, p. 60.)

to translate aftir the sentence, and not oneli aftir the wordis, so that the sentence be as opin, either openere, in English as in Latyn, and go not fer fro the lettre; and if the lettre may not be suid in the translating, let the sentence euere be hool and open, for the wordis owen to serue to the entent and sentence, and ellis the wordis ben superflu either false.[1]

This emphasis on the 'openness' of meaning is one of the most essential tenets of the Bible translator. The instruction of the layman by opening to him an accurate and reliable version of the Scriptures was the very mainspring of the whole movement. Accuracy of translation achieved at the expense of simplicity would defeat the whole end and aim of men such as Wycliffe and his successors, Erasmus, More and Tyndale. The fault of following the Latin too closely spoilt the first Wycliffite translation and had to be remedied in the second recension. Translators of the Early Tudor period benefited by the general attitude towards language during the early years of the sixteenth century. Standard speech, 'a selection of the language really used by men,' was being established and an increasing sense of linguistic propriety helps them to avoid the faults of the earlier translators. Miles Coverdale, who continued the work set on foot by Tyndale, had this linguistic sense highly developed. In 1535 he produced a translation from the German and Latin, which, in its second edition, was formally sanctioned by the king's licence. The care with which he went about his activities is the outcome of a highly self-conscious attitude to linguistic study. He claims both accuracy of translation and ease of style:

> ... I haue not in any poynte gone from the true meanynge of the authoure, but haue tho-rowly obserued the phrases of both tongues, auoydynge in all that I myght the darke ma-ner of translatynge after the latine phrases, to the intente the Englyshe reader myghte haue the full vnderstandynge hereof wythout anye knowledge of the latyne tongue.[2]

[1] *Ibid.*, p. 57.
[2] Preface to translation of Calvin's work on the Sacrament, *A faythful and moste godly treatyse concernynge the most sacred sacrament of the blessed body and bloude of our Saviour Christ* (1550), sig. A.ii.

EARLY TUDOR CRITICISM

Behind his translation of the Bible of 1535 lies a long process of selection and comparison. He says:

> To help me herein I have had sundry translations, not only in Latin, but also of the Dutch interpretors, whom because of their singular gifts and special diligence in the Bible, I have been the more glad to follow for the most part according as I was required.[1]

The purpose of this meticulous care was to qualify the translators to choose the style best suited to their audience and yet not offensive to their translator's conscience. The creation of a serviceable plain style rather than 'elegancie of speche'[2] is their aim, because

> there was a speciall regard to be had to the rude and vnlettred people, who perchaunce through default of atteigning to the high stile, should also thereby haue been defrauded of the profit and fruicte of vnderstandyng the sence, whiche thing that thei might dooe, was the onely purpose why it was first translated.[3]

Throughout the Early Tudor period, when discussion of Bible translation becomes as common 'as though it were but a Canterburye tale,'[4] the same problems are debated and the same methods are chosen. As scholarship increases, the translation of the Bible benefits by restored knowledge and sharper perspicuity. Whether early or late in the period there is little difference in the fundamental approach to the subject. William Whittingham, revising a version of the New Testament in 1557, uses the same methods as Tyndale and Coverdale before him:

> First as touching the perusing of the text, it was diligently reuised by the moste approued Greke examples, and conference

---

[1] Prologue to Tyndale's translation of the Bible, 1535.
[2] Nicholas Udall, *op. cit.*, Preface to the Reader.
[3] *Ibid*.
Cf. *A discourse wherein is debated whether it be expedient that the Scripture should be in English for al men to reade that wyll*. Anonymous (1554):
'... hardnes in scripture ofte doeth arise of the proprietie of the tongue, that euerye tongue hath his owne proper phrase not perfitlye to bee knowen beinge translated into another tongue.' Sig. C vi^r, ll. 11–18.
[4] *A discourse wherein is debated*, etc.

THE TRANSLATION OF THE BIBLE

of translations in other tonges as the learned may easiely iudge, both by the faithful rendering of the sentence, and also by the proprietie of the wordes and perspicuitie of the phrase. . . . And because the Hebrew and Greke phrases which are strange to rendre in other tongues, and also shorte, shulde not be so harde, I haue sometyme interpreted them without any whit diminishing the grace of the sense, as our la*n*gage doth vse them. . . .[1]

Thus the Early Tudor period sees the fulfilment of many attempts to establish a vernacular version of the Bible. The men of this time are conscious that they have been preceded by many similar workers,[2] but that there has never been so concerted an effort as in their age. There was a combination of conditions as propitious for this branch of the translating activity as for secular translation. The coincidence of the revival of classical studies and the Reformation produced a new attitude to the usefulness of knowledge to individuals. Secular knowledge was adjudged to be a necessary part of the rounded, fully-developed personality. The resources of classical knowledge were therefore thrown open by means of translation to everyone who wished to assimilate them without having the means of reading the originals. Similarly, the leading spirits of the Reformation asserted the right of the individual to have access to Scriptural knowledge. A careful translation was therefore imperative to supply the needs of an eager and receptive audience.[3] A tract of 1539 goes so far as to say that the reading of the Bible has displaced the romances:

---

[1] Quoted A. W. Pollard, *op. cit.*, p. 26.

[2] E.g. Anonymous, *A compendious old treatyse shewynge howe that we ought to haue ye scripture in Englysshe* (1530) : '. . . venerabilis Bede ledde by the spirite of gode trãslated a greate parte of the byble into englyche. Whose originalles ben in many abbeys in yngland. . . .' Thomas Cranmer, in the Preface to the Great Bible, published by royal authority and under his direction in 1539, refers to the Saxon translations. *The Fathers of the English Church*, Vol. 3, 'Various Tracts and Extracts from the Works of Thomas Cranmer' (1809), p. 56.

[3] Foxe, speaking of this period, says:
'. . . great multitudes . . . tasted and followed the sweetness of God's Holy Word almost in as ample manner, for the number of well disposed hearts, as now . . . Certes, the fervent zeal of those Christian days seemed much superior to these our days and times, as manifestly may appear by their sitting up all night in reading and hearing: also by their expenses and charges in buying of books in English. . . .' *Actes and Monumentes*, 4, 217, ff.

EARLY TUDOR CRITICISM

Englishmen have now in hand in every Church and place, almost every man the Holy Bible and New Testament in their mother tongue instead of the old fabulous and fantastical books of the Table Round, Launcelot du Lac &c., and such other, whose unpure filth and vain fabulocity the light of God has abolished utterly.[1]

With the awakening of national consciousness in the later Middle Ages, the translators of the Bible were stimulated by the fact that other countries possessed versions in their several vernaculars. Purvey remarks in his Prologue that

> Frenshe men, Beemers, and Britons han the bible, and othere bokis of deuocioun and of exposicioun, translatid in here modir langage; whi shulden not English men haue the same in here modir langage, I can not wite....[2]

His opinion is repeated by Coverdale in the sixteenth century:

> But to saye the trueth before God, it was nether my laboure ner desyre, to haue this worke put in my hande: neuertheles it greued me that other natyons shulde be more plenteously prouyded for with the scripture in theyr mother tongue, then we.[3]

The translator has high status in the ranks of those who render service to the state and discharge an important office in the Tudor period. Udall is very conscious of the position of all who undertake the work of translation:

> It is therefore no smal benefite that suche persones dooe to a common weale, whiche are willinglye trauailers in this kinde of writing. For as for newe bookes of trifleing vanities and profane argumentes we nede none, there are daily so many written: but to haue such woorkes made common to the publique vse of ye vnlearned multitude, as are the principall beste, and haue

---

[1] 'A Summary Declaration of the Faith, Uses and Observations in England.' Collier, *Ecclesiastical History*, 2, Collection of Records, 47.
[2] See Forshall and Madden, *op. cit.*, Preface, p. 59.
Cf. also Purvey's English version of treatise on the debate on biblical translations between the Lollard, Peter Payne, and the Dominican, Thomas Palmer, at Oxford, 1403-1405. M. Deanesly, *op. cit.*, Appendix 2, p. 441.
[3] Prologue to translation of the Bible (1535), Pollard, *op. cit.*, p. 203.

THE TRANSLATION OF THE BIBLE

been written by noble Clerkes of vndoubted learnyng, knowelage, and godlinesse, therein consisteth suche a publique benefite as ... is in mine estimacion, woorthie publique thankes and regarde.[1]

At every stage the work of the Bible translators is the subject of fierce controversy, involving scholars and men of letters as well as theologians and divines. No question of their aim or method is left unprobed, and the mass of comment is organized against opposition more clearly than ever became necessary for secular translation. The unanimity of their comments and the resemblance of these opinions to those advanced by secular translators show that translators in both fields were working with a common critical intention.

[1] *Op. cit.*, Vol. 1, Preface, 'Unto the Kinges Maiestie.'

CHAPTER III
SECULAR TRANSLATION AND TRANSLATORS

WITH multifarious interests to examine and compare, writers of the sixteenth century needed the help of some definite system or touchstone by which to measure the potentialities of the English language. This need is in part supplied by the discipline of translation from both classical and contemporary vernacular languages. The mass of comment contained in prefaces, dedications and *obiter dicta* in the Early Tudor period shows that the translators conceived of their work as a literary exercise calling for critical method and decision. This material contributes valuable evidence of literary and linguistic taste and clarifies many contemporary opinions concerning the value of English as a literary language.

A critical decision is presupposed in the translator's choice of model. Didactic or moral value of subject matter is their first consideration, which lays great responsibility upon the method of translation. The transposition of the material into other terms must be accomplished without damaging its integrity. The translator must then consider which method will the better serve his purposes. A literal translation might maintain the close connection between original and translation. On the other hand, a paraphrase into the idiom of the second language might convey the meaning more clearly and cogently. The translator who has any sense of his duty can hardly evade the making of a decision on these points. He is then confronted with the choice of the style which will best meet the demands of the audience to whom it is addressed. Care for the value of the subject matter makes obscurity undesirable, since the work must be easily understood by all readers. At the same time, the diction and style must be approved by more scholarly standards and the reconciliation of these claims presents another problem for the translator's consideration.

SECULAR TRANSLATION AND TRANSLATORS

The extent to which these principles were consistently or successfully applied by the translators of the Early Tudor and Elizabethan periods is a separate study, so, for the purposes of tracing the growth of criticism, consideration will be restricted to their theory alone. The translators have no doubt about the importance of their task. Scholarly culture had become an essential attribute of the Renascence courtier and man of affairs. It had become part of the framework on which to build up a complete and useful personality. A national programme demanded its extension to the less learned, who could only approach it by versions in their mother tongue. The translators' recognition of the need for disseminating knowledge is reiterated in their prefaces. If the literature of entertainment reaches this public in the vernacular, so also may more useful knowledge. It may be a collection of legal knowledge,

> cōpounded both in English and in Latyne, to ye intent it may be the easelyer taken and perceyued of them that are but meanely learned in the Latyne tonge....[1]

or of moral precepts for the better conduct of man's life, which

> for this his excellencie deserueth not onely of the Grecians, and Latinistes to bee read and knowen, but also to bee translated into the Vulgare toungue of all nacions.[2]

---

[1] Thomas Phaer, *A newe boke of Presidentes* (1543), Preface, sig. A.ii.
Cf. also Sir Thomas Elyot, *The Doctrinal of Princes made by the noble oratour Isocrates* (1534). Elyot translates 'to the intent that thei, which do not vnderstande greeke nor latine, shoulde not lack the commoditee and pleasure, whiche maie be taken in readyng thereof.' (Preface, sig. Aiiᵛ.)
Leonard Cox, *Arte or Crafte of Rhethoryke* (between 1527 and 1530), ed. F. I. Carpenter (1899), p. 42:
'... trustynge therby to do some pleasure and case to suche as haue by neclygence or els fals parsuasyons be put to the lernynge of other scyences or euer [A. iii. b] they haue attayned any meane knowledge of the latyne tongue.'
Thomas Phaer, *The Regiment of Life, wherunto is added a treatise of the pestilence, with the boke of children* (1545):
'... but my pur-pose is here ... to distribut in Englishe to them that are vnlerned, part of ye treasure that is in other lāguages, to prouoke them that are of better learnīg, to vtter theyr knowlege in such lyke attemptes:...' Preface, sig. Aiiᵛ.
[2] Robert Burrant, *Preceptes of Cato with annotacions of D. Erasmus of Roterodame very profitable for all menne* (1553), sig. A iiᵛ.

43

EARLY TUDOR CRITICISM

The work of Erasmus, the man who is held by his contemporaries to be the peer of the ancients,

> the mā, to whom in lerning no liuynge man may hym selfe compare: and nat onely passeth them that be alyue but also from the most parte of olde autors hath beraft the price,[1]

has such moral value that translation was imperative.[2] Latin, the once natural medium of a cosmopolitan scholar, was now felt to be restrictive. To be adequately accessible the work of Erasmus must appear in the vernacular, dedicated to 'such as are not lerned in the latin tonge.'[3]

The use of the English language to convey by translation such a variety of knowledge is a tribute to its status as a medium for serious literature, for

> yf other bokes which are made eyther for delyte and pleasure of the eares, as are rymes, iestes, and suche other, or for the memorial of thynges that are gone and past, as storycs, chronicles and lyke, are had in estimation,[4]

the translators' carefully chosen work is by its excellence even more worthy of esteem.

They all endorse Thomas Paynell's plea for the effective circulation of literature:

> ... what auayleth hit / to haue golde or abundance of riches / if one can nat use hit? What helpeth costely medicines / if one re-ceyue them nat? So what profiteth us a boke / be hit neuer so expedient and frutefull / if we vnder-stande hit nat? ...[5]

The translators felt that they could render service to the state by working in the vernacular. During the early years of the Tudor period, England, unrent by political differences after the Wars of the Roses, was able to gather her forces and measure herself against other European nations. The spirit

---
[1] Gentian Hervet, *De Immensa Dei Misericordia* (1533), Preface, sig. A ii^v–A iii^r.
[2] *Ibid.*: 'And where as afore lerned men only dyd get out bothe pleasure and great frute in redynge of this boke, nowe euery man as welle rude as lerned may haue this sermō of the mercy of god as cōmon vnto him as the mercy of god it selfe is.' Sig. A ii^r-v.
[3] Edmonde Becke, translation of *Two dyaloges wrytten in laten by the famous clerke D. Erasmus of Roterodame* ... (1549), Preface.
[4] Thomas Phaer, *A newe boke of Presidentes* (1543), a. iiv.
[5] Translation of the *Regimen Sanitatis Salerni* (1528). Prefatory letter.

44

SECULAR TRANSLATION AND TRANSLATORS

of emulation was a stimulus to literary activity in the vernacular. The translators express their shame that other countries have greater achievements in this genre:

> For what Royalme almoste (Englande excepted), hath not all the good autours that euer wrote translated into the mother tounge. . . . ?[1]

A similar transference of knowledge by means of translation had been made by the Romans from Greek literature and a similar transference was proved possible in the sixteenth century world by the example of

> frenche men, Italions, and Germanes, to our no litle reproche for our negligence and slouth.[2]

Just as the advocates of pure Ciceronianism tried to justify their opinions by their desire to reproduce classical achievement, the English translators find more recent exemplars to rouse ambition in vernacular work. Hoby speaks for the pride of them all when he urges translation so that

> we alone of the worlde maye not bee styll counted barbarous in oure tunge, as in time out of minde we have bene in our maners. And so shall we perchaunce in time become as famouse in Englande, as the learned men of other nations have ben and presently are.[3]

England is at this time avid to receive all supplies of new knowledge which the translators can provide and claims to be by no means inferior in intellectual power to other nations. Sir Thomas Wilson states his conviction that

> the Englisch naciō is so pregnaunt and quicke to achiue any kynde, or Arte, of knowlege, whereunto wit maie attain, that they are not inferiour to any other: . . .[4]

He shares also the competitive spirit of the time,

---

[1] Nicholas Udall, *op. cit.*, Vol. 1, Preface 'Unto the Kinges Maiestie.'
[2] Sir Thomas Elyot, *The Boke named the Gouernour*, ed. H. H. S. Croft (1883), Vol. 1, p. 269. All further references will be to this edition.
[3] Letter to Lord Hastings, prefixed to Hoby's translation from the Italian of Castiglione, *The Book of The Courtier* (1561), ed. W. Raleigh (1900), p. 9. This edition has been quoted throughout these studies.
[4] *The rule of Reason, conteinyng the Arte of Logique, set forth in Englishe* (1551), 'The Epistle to the Kyng,' sig. A iii^{r-v}.

EARLY TUDOR CRITICISM

farther pōdering that diuerse learned mē of other coūtreis haue heretofore for the furtheraunce of knowlege, not suffred any of the Sciences liberal to be hidden in the Greke, or Latine tongue, but haue with most earnest trauaile made euery of them familiar to their vulgare people. . . .[1]

Although the translators were sure of a public eager to receive their work, they did not escape stimulating opposition. The obscurantist tendency which Cheke encountered in his controversy with Gardiner strongly resisted the attempts of the translators to lay open to all men knowledge which had formerly been the prerogative of the learned. It is of men of the calibre of Gardiner and his supporters that Hoby speaks when he says that

> our men weene it sufficient to have a perfecte knowledge, to no other ende, but to profite themselves, and (as it were) after much paynes in breaking up a gap, bestow no lesse to close it up again. . . .[2]

Such men had only destructive criticism to contribute, the carping of such

> curyous, fantasticall parsons, priyuey dyffamours of dylygent and vertuous laboure, who, though they them self to theyr reproche do ydely or with silence passe theyr tyme, be yet greuously pynched wyth enuye that other shulde trauayle to vtter theyr talente to the commodytie of many. . . .[3]

Translation, with its responsibility towards the general welfare of people unable to derive benefit from classical knowledge in the original, its position as one of the main channels for disseminating this knowledge and its vaunted capacity to reinstate English prestige in the world of letters must be considered as one of the most important of Early Tudor interests.

[1] *Ibid.*, sig. A iii[v]. [2] *Op. cit.*, p. 8.
[3] T. Nicolls, *The hystory writtone by Thucidides . . . translated out of Frenche into the Englysh language . . .* (1550). 'To the right worshypfull Mayster John Cheke . . .' sig. A. iii[r].
  Cf. also Thomas Phaer, *The Regiment of Life* (1545).
'If they knowe better, let vs haue parte: yf they doe not, why repine they at me? why condemne they the thinge that they can not amēd or yf they can, why dissimule they theyr cōnyng? how long wold they haue the people ignoraunt? why grutch they phisike to come forth in Englysshe? wolde they haue no man to knowe but onely they?' Preface, sig. A iii[r].

SECULAR TRANSLATION AND TRANSLATORS

Conscious of the novelty of their enterprise, the translators feel bound to apologize for any ineptitude which their work may betray. Their fruit is

> of a straunge kynde (such as no Englishe grounde hath before this time, and in this sorte by any tyllage brought forth),[1]

and may therefore seem at first 'somewhat rough, and harshe in the mouth.'[2] Expressions like this point to a phase of indecision, not unfruitful for criticism, but demanding, for increased effectiveness, the integration of opinions into an ordered scheme. There was in England no Etienne Dolet to draw up a programme on the model of *La Manière de bien traduire d'une langue en aultre* (1540), but the unanimity in the comments of English translators indicates the acceptance of some general standards.

The translator must cultivate 'the exquisite diligence of an interpretour'[3] since care for his subject matter is essential. Whatever the method finally chosen may be,

> yet doeth none willinglye swerue or dissente from the minde and sence of his autoure. Albeit some gre more nere to the wordes of the lettre, and some vse the libertie of translating at large, not so precisely binding themselues to the streight interpretacion of euery woorde and sillable, (so the sence bee kepte: (yet doe thei all agree) euerye one as his veine serueth hym) in feithfullye rendryng the sence of their booke.[4]

This responsibility towards the original shows a literary conscience which had been dormant during the mediaeval period. Writers of the Middle Ages had no sense of copyright, but drew freely upon a common treasury of material, to be incorporated and adapted without acknowledgement. A new approach to classical literature in the Renascence period had produced in men of letters an appreciation of the individual character of each author. The translators were forced to assess this and preserve it as far as was possible in

---

[1] Wilson, *Rule of Reason*, 'Epistle to the Kynge,' sig. A. iiv.
[2] *Ibid*.
[3] Sir Thomas Elyot, *The Education or bringing vp of Children* (1535), sig. A. v.
[4] Nicholas Udall, *op. cit.*, Vol. 1, Preface 'To the moste vertuous Ladye Quene Katerine...'

EARLY TUDOR CRITICISM

the idiom of a different language. Their preliminary choice of author made and his particular value for subject matter decided, attention was again focussed on the language. Out of the comparison of the language of the original and that of the translator arises a sense of the essential character of both. The integrity of the language as well as that of the author and his matter must be considered. Here again the translators are aware that they are attempting a new kind of work and that an advance has been made upon previous tradition. Their predecessors, they thought, had little

> respecte to the obseruacyō of the thyng which in translacyō is of all other most necessary and requisite, that is to saye, to rendre the sence [*and*] the very meanyng of the author....
>
> The lerned knoweth *th*at euery tonge hathe his peculyer proprietie, phrase, maner of locucion, enargies and vehemēcie, which so aptlie in any other tōg cannot be expressed.[1]

This sense of language is developed in all the men who seriously undertook translation as a literary duty and discipline in France as well as in England. Dolet lays down as the third rule of translation the injunction that

> the translator must not translate literally word for word, but so that the meaning of the author shall be expressed, due regard being paid to the idioms of both languages.[2]

He is thus of Du Bellay's conviction that 'chacune langue a je ne sçay quoi propre seulement à elles.'[3]

The translators of the Early Tudor period work with a similar principle in mind. They realize that a rendering too strictly literal tends to impair the intrinsic value of the finished product both for the value of the matter and of the style in English. If too much attention is paid to a word-for-word reproduction, both aims are defeated, for

> so the sence of the author is oftentimes corrupted *an*d depraued,

---

[1] Edmonde Becke, *op. cit.*, Preface to the Reader.
[2] See R. C. Christie, *Etienne Dolet* (1899), pp. 356-357.
[3] *Défense et Illustration de la Langue Françoyse*, ed. Léon Séché (1925), p. 173.

SECULAR TRANSLATION AND TRANSLATORS

and neyther the grace of the one tonge nor yet of the other is truely obserued or aptlie expressed.[1]

Translation lays as much emphasis upon a sensitive study of the character of the English language as upon exactitudes of meaning in the original. It promotes careful study of the diction and structure of the language, disciplined by comparison with that of the original, whether Latin, Greek, or European vernacular. In this respect, the exercise of translation may be said to have brought about a study of language which is essentially critical.

Elyot claims considerable strenuousness for his methods,

> ... not supersticiousely folowynge the letter ... but kepynge the sentence [i.e. *sententia*] and intent of the Autour I haue attemted (not with lyttell study) to reduce into english the right phrase or forme of speakyng.[2]

His critical sense is developed to a degree remarkable for his time. He consciously compares the qualities of the languages from which he translates, is careful for the idiom of each and aims at the ultimate benefit of the English language. For his translation from Isocrates he uses both the Greek and Latin versions

> to thintent onely that I wolde assaie, if our Englisshe tunge mought receiue the quicke and propre sentences pronounced by the greekes. And in this experience I haue founde (if I be not muche deceiued) that the forme of speakyng, vsed of the Greekes, called in greeke, and also in latine, *Phrasis*, muche nere approcheth to that, whiche at this daie we vse: than the order of the latine tunge: I meane in the sentences, and not in the wordes: whiche I doubte not shall be affirmed by them, who sufficiently instructed in all the saide three tunges, shall with a good iudgement read this worke....[3]

[1] Edmonde Becke, *op. cit.*, Preface to the Reader.
Cf. Du Bellay: '... il est impossible de le rendre avecques la mesme grace dont l'auteur en a usé ... [et] ... si vous efforcez exprimer le naïf dans une autre langue, observant la loi de traduire, qui est n'espacier point hors des limites de l'auteur, votre diction sera contrainte, froide et de mauvaise grace.' *Op. cit.*, p. 73.
[2] Preface to the translation of *A svvete and devovte sermon of holy saynt Ciprian of mortalitie of man* (1534), sig. A iii ʳ & ᵛ.
[3] *The Doctrinal of Princes made by the noble oratour Isocrates* (1534), 'Sir Thomas Elio knight to the reader.' sig. A. ii ʳ⁻ᵛ.

EARLY TUDOR CRITICISM

The significance of this claim to a comparative study of English and the classical languages lies in the new direction given to scholarship. The vernacular is now considered important enough to be compared with Greek and Latin and is admitted to show to some advantage in the comparison. Praise for 'a faithfull, [and] sure enterpretacion . . . ought to be takē for the greatest praise of all'[1] and this can only be achieved by a thorough preliminary grasp of concrete varieties of idiom.

The work of the translators is submitted to the scrutiny and judgment of the learned. Trying

> to interprete and turne the Latine into Englyshe with as muche grace of our vulgare toung, as in [their] slendre power and knowelage hath lyen,[2]

the translators demand the application of these scholarly standards. Their work must undergo careful correction such as that described by John Harington:

> I caused it to be conferred with the latine auctor, and so by the knowen wel lerned to be corrected: after whose handelyng me thought a new spirite and life was geuen it, and many partes semed as it were with a new cote araied, as well for the orderly placyng and eloquently changeyng of some woordes, as also for the plainly openyng and learnedly amending of the sence.[3]

Similarly Nicolls addresses his translation of Thucydides to Cheke:

> Requyryng you of your accustomed benignyte, not onely with fauoure to accepte this the furste my fruict in translatyon but also conferringe it with the Greke, so to amende and correct it, in those places and sentences, whiche youre exacte lernynge and knolaige shall Iudge mete to be altered and refourmed, that thereby thys sayd translation may triumphantly resist and wyth-

---

[1] Nicholas Grimald, *Marcvs Tullius Ciceroes three bookes of dueties* (edition of 1558), Preface.
[2] Nicholas Udall, *Apophthegmes . . . First gathered and compiled in Latin by the right famous clerke Maister Erasmus of Roterodame* (1542), Preface, sig. 2ᵛ.
[3] John Harington the Elder, *The booke of freendeship of Marcus Tullie Cicero* (1550), Preface, sig. A. iiiiʳ.

SECULAR TRANSLATION AND TRANSLATORS

stande the malycyous and deadly stynge of the generall and most ennemyes of all good exercyse.[1]

The finished product should be equally valuable as an accurate translation of the matter and as a piece of work not incongruous with the native genius of the English language.

Just as translation is recognized as the product of a mind working according to a critical system, the response it awakens in an attentive and scholarly reader was likewise to be a critical one. It should be a means of training linguistic discrimination and an incentive to close study of both original and translation. If a work of this kind should

> happe into a good students hand: hee will not think it ynough to runne ouer it once: as we fare with trifles, and toyes: but aduisedly, and with good leasure, three, or foure, or fiue tymes, he will reade it, and reade it, and reade it agayne: first, by the principall pointes, by the definitions, and the deuisions: to see, what is treated, how farre forthe, in what order, and with what varietie: then, to mark the preceptes, reasons, conclusions & common places: after, vnto the sayde places to referre all the stories, with the verses poeticall: finally, as well in the englysh, as the latine, to weygh well properties of wordes, fashions of phrases, and the ornamentes of both.[2]

Translation is critical in itself and the cause that criticism is in other men.

Since the translators are pre-occupied with the formulation of stylistic and linguistic principles, they naturally refer to the topic which approached most nearly to a codified system of language, that of rhetoric. The aim of rhetoric being to achieve a given effect in the most appropriate language, it coincided with the main direction of translation. The application of the rules of rhetoric to translation is specifically made by Grimald:

> Howbeit loke, what rule the Rhetoricia giues in precept, to be obserued of an Oratour, in telling of his tale: [tha]t it be short, & without ydle words: [tha]t it be playn, & without dark sence: that it bee prouable, & without any swaruinge from the

---

[1] Op cit., Prefatory letter, sig. A iii^r. [2] Grimald, *Ciceroes Dueties*, Preface.

trouthe: the same rule should be vsed in examining, & iudging of trāslation. For if it be not as brief, as the verie authors text requireth: what so is added to his perfite stile, shall appere superfluous, & to serue rather to the making of some paraphrase, or commentarie. Therto, if it be vttered wi*th* ynkehorne termes, & not with vsuall wordes: or if it be phrased *wi*[*th*] wrasted or farrefetched fourmes of speeche: not fine, but harshe, not easie, but hard, not natural, but violent,[1]

the translation will be a failure. This measuring of translation by the rules of rhetoric proves that the translators felt the need to express their critical decisions in some ordered form.

The problems of the style to be chosen for translation are hotly debated by rhetoricians and men of letters throughout the Early Tudor period. Although they are convinced

> the cunning is no lesse, and the prayse as great . . . to translate any thing excellently into Englishe, as into any other language,[2]

they are none the less aware that the English language was as yet untried for their purposes and somewhat crude compared with the classical languages from which so much of their translation was made. They persevere, nevertheless, hoping that

> after a little vse, and familiar accustomyng thereunto . . . the same wil ware euery one daie more pleasant then other.[3]

Elyot finds that the classical authors address themselves

> incomparably with more grace and delectation to the reder than our englisshe tonge may yet comprehende[4]

and Sir Thomas Wyatt, in an early and little known translation, experiences the same difficulty in translating Plutarch:

> And after I had made a profe of nyne or ten Dialogues / the labour began to seme tedious / by sup[*er*]fluous often rehersyng of one thyng. which tho pauenture in the latyn shal be laudable

---
[1] *Ibid.*
[2] Wilson, *Translation of Demosthenes* (1570), 'The Epistle to the right Honorable Sir William Cecill, Knight . . .', sig. i[r].
[3] Wilson, *Rule of Reason*, 'Epistle to the Kyng,' sig.A. ii[v].–A. ii[r].
[4] *Gouvernour*, Vol. 1, p. 129.

SECULAR TRANSLATION AND TRANSLATORS

/ by plentuous diuersite of the spekyng of it (for I wyll nat that my iugement shall disalowe in any thyng so approued an auctour) yet for lacke of suche diuersyte in our tong / it shulde want a great dele of the grace....[1]

The translators choose the plain style. Because of their obligations to their unlearned audience and the value of their material, they had to be guiltless of obscurity or undue cultivation of style at the expense of matter. Their work had to be comprehensible to those who needed it most and the translators must

> with more exact diligence conforme the style therof with the phrase of our englishe, desiringe more to make it playne to all readers, than to flourishe it with ouer moch eloquence....[2]

Their unlearned readers will not be able to judge of the merits of the translation by comparison with the original, but will have to accept it at its face value as easily understood and useful. John Harington the Elder explains how much this consideration weighs with him:

> ... how so euer it shalbe liked of the learned, I hope it shalbe allowed of the vnlatined. Whose capacitees by my owne I cōsider, and for lacke of a fine and flowing stile, I haue vsed the plaine and common speache.[3]

The use of the plain style is therefore a conscious choice, part of the 'duetie of a translatour.'[4] The translators' usage reinforces the attempts made in other intellectual spheres in the sixteenth century—by the Cambridge circle, by the Bible translators and by the rhetoricians—to build up a standard English language for literary purposes, clear, lucid and workmanlike. The aureate style is rejected at a time when ornate speech was still counted a flourishing fashion and 'to ouerflouryshe wyth superfluous speach' could be an author's claim to 'be counted equall with the

---

[1] Translation of *Plutarch Quyete of Mynde* (1527), ed. C. R. Baskervill (Harvard University Press, 1931). Address to 'the most excellent and most v[er]rtuous princes Katheryn/ quene of Englande and of Fraunce...' sig. a ii r.
[2] Sir Thomas Elyot, *The Image of Governance* (1551), Preface, sig. A ii v.
[3] *Op. cit.*, 'To the ... duchesse of Suffolke,' sig. A. iii v.
[4] Udall, *Apophthegmes*..., Preface, sig. ii v.

EARLY TUDOR CRITICISM

best that euer wrote Englysh.'[1] Their choice needs comment and explanation, since it is in the nature of a novelty.

Sir Thomas Wilson apologizes because he rejects Ciceronian eloquence. He feels that it is better to write

> plainely & nakedly after the common sort of men in few words, than to ouerflowe wyth vnnecessarie and superfluous eloquence as Cicero is thought sometimes to doe: But perhaps wheras I haue bene somewhat curious to followe Demosthenes naturall phrase, it may be thought that I doe speake ouer bare Englysh, well I had rather follow his veyne, the whych was to speake simply and plainly to the comōn peoples vnderstanding.[2]

The aims of the translators as regards choice of style are clearly formulated and they write according to carefully considered tenets. The principles of rhetoric confirm their opinion and the unanimity of the translators' comments shows how definite their standards had become. Theirs was 'a common woorke of buildyng.'[3]

The ramifications of the translators' problems extend into the controversies on diction which raged in the Early Tudor period and throw extra weight upon the side of the men opposed to the fashion of 'inkhorn' terms. Their fundamental aim being clarity and the preservation of the character of the English language, they submit their diction to the test of these requirements. On them rests much of the responsibility for the control of borrowings and new formations from other languages. It was fortunate for the language that this responsibility was laid upon men who exercised discretion and moderation in augmenting the vocabulary. Translation from the wealth of subject matter in classical languages was a searching test of the resources of the English language and it was inevitable that in some respects it should be found inadequate. Equivalents could not always be found for the complexity and subtlety of expression of the classics. Gavin Douglas found that

---

[1] Wilson, *Translation of Demosthenes*, Preface, fol. 8ᵛ.
[2] *Ibid.*
[3] Udall, *Paraphrases of Erasmus*, Preface 'Unto the Reader', Vol. 1.

SECULAR TRANSLATION AND TRANSLATORS

> ... thar bene Latyne wordis mony ane,
> That in our leid ganand translatioun hes nane
> Les than we menis thar sentence and grauite
> And ȝit scant weill exponit.[1]

Sir Thomas Elyot, explaining a system of education largely drawn from Latin sources, especially from Quintilian, is unable to find a translation of the many technical words required, and is therefore occasionally

> constrained to usurpe a latine worde, ... whiche worde, though it be strange and darke, yet by declaring the vertue in a fewe mo wordes, the name ones brought in custome shall be as facile to understande as other wordes late commen out of Italy and Fraunce, and made denizins amonge us.[2]

These foreign elements, valuable if they can enrich the English language by extending its powers of expression, must be easily acceptable as 'denizins' by general usage. No legitimate means of raising the status of the English language could be rejected at a time when all the vernaculars were vying with each other in the race for classical excellence. A judicious adoption of new words was a valuable source of new vitality, provided that these words were

> by the sufferaunce of wise men nowe receiued by custome, wherby the terme shall be made familiare.[3]

The selection of such words calls for the use of sound stylistic judgment, a sensitive perception of shades of meaning and aptness of expression and Sir Thomas Elyot does not make innovations in language without careful study. Argument such as that upon the relative meanings of 'intellect' and 'intelligence'[4] is proof of his care to express the niceties of the Latin as exactly as possible in English. He coins words to

> thentent to ornate our langage with usinge wordes in their propre signification. Wherof what commoditie may ensue all wise men wyll, I dought nat, consider.[5]

The problems of translation were not in themselves new.

---

[1] *Op. cit.*, Vol. 2, p. 14, ll. 31–p. 15, l. 2.   [2] *Gouernour*, Vol. 1, p. 243.
[3] *Ibid.*, Vol. I, p. 268.   [4] *Ibid.*, Vol. 2, pp. 373–375.   [5] *Ibid.*, Vol. 2, p. 369.

EARLY TUDOR CRITICISM

Roman civilization had desired to transfer the body of Greek knowledge into its mother tongue and the transmission of knowledge had continued at a varying pace ever since. Alfred in the Anglo-Saxon period cited the long tradition behind the translators' activity[1] and had discussed aims and methods.[2] There had always been the need of giving the lay people moral and religious instruction in their mother tongue and the demands for simple, lucid language were the same.[3] It is, however, during the late fifteenth and early sixteenth centuries that for the first time translation becomes the *locus* for careful literary and linguistic discussion. Whether the translators are men of no considerable qualifications, such as Caxton, or of remarkable intellectual power such as the men of the Cambridge circle, Ascham, Elyot, Wilson, and their source of inspiration, Cheke, 'a man of men, supernaturally traded in al tongues',[4] they all reflect the many linguistic interests of their age. They discuss and select the best among these fashions for a concerted attempt to reinstate English among the vernaculars as capable of receiving the mass of knowledge opened up by the classical studies of the Renascence period. Since it was the layman's approach to a treasury which had been open before to scholars only, it ranked very high among the interests of the Tudor period. It was

> learning it self, and a great staye to youth, and the noble ende to the whiche they oughte to applie their wittes, that with diligence and studye have attained a perfect understanding, to open a gap for others to followe their steppes, and a vertuous exercise for the unlatined to come by learning, and to fill their minde with the morall vertues, and their body with civyll condicions.[5]

[1] Preface to WS. Version of Gregory's *Cura Pastoralis*, ed. H. Sweet, *Anglo-Saxon Reader* (1928), p. 6, ll. 54–60.
[2] *Ibid.*, p. 7, ll. 74–82.
[3] E.g. Richard Rolle, Preface to *The English Psalter* (c. 1338), ed. Hope Emily Allen (1931), p. 7, l. 91 ff. Cf. also Trevisa's *Dialogue between a Lord and a Clerk concerning translation*, ed. A. W. Pollard, *Fifteenth Century Prose and Verse* (1903), pp. 203 ff.
[4] Thomas Nash, Preface to Greene's *Menaphon* (1589), ed. Gregory Smith *Elizabethan Critical Essays* (1904), p. 313.
[5] Sir Thomas Hoby, 'Letter to the right honorable The Lord Henry Hastings...' prefixed to *The Courtier*, p. 9.

SECULAR TRANSLATION AND TRANSLATORS

The invention of printing had made possible the wider circulation of the classics, in the original and in translation, thus making the work of the translators effective and influential. Books and manuscripts circulated rapidly with the incessant comings and goings of scholars between England and the Continent and men of letters seized every opportunity of annexing more knowledge for the vernacular by means of translation. Sometimes, in the maelstrom of this intellectual commerce, contingencies arose which were not propitious for the leisured art of translation, as when Elyot was prevented from finishing his translation of the *Image of Governance* because 'the owner . . . importunately called for his boke.'[1] Such hindrances were rare and translation quickened the pulse of culture considerably.

Consideration of the opinions underlying this scattered material shows that the translators were keenly conscious of what they were doing. They made important decisions about their choice of method and style, of which the validity was upheld by the coincidence of rhetorical precept with the independent decisions which emerged from the controversies of men of letters. The moving spirits of the translating activity were the men most influential in the Early Tudor intellectual world, Cheke and the Cambridge circle, men of comprehensive abilities. It was inevitable that they should, in stimulating translation, raise it to the status of applied criticism. Since it fostered linguistic and literary judgment, had an ordered system of style and method, explored the resources of the English language and augmented them where necessary, translation made an invaluable contribution to the training of critical habit. It touches upon urgent linguistic problems of the day and the later development of the language owes much to the good sense and discrimination of those who submitted it to a careful discipline before its potentialities had been thoroughly gauged.

[1] Preface, sig. a ii^r.

CHAPTER IV

EDUCATION: TUTOR AND SCHOOLMASTER

MANY of the literary and linguistic activities of the Early Tudor period depend upon the response of individuals to the stimulus of new ideas and produce quick results, as in the mass of translation and comment, or in creative work which shows the grasp of new method and conviction. Education, on the contrary, is very largely crystallized in institutions. As each institution has its own vulnerability or resistance to new ideas, the changes in intellectual approach which took place in this field are more variable and difficult to ascertain than in less conservative spheres.

Education in the fifteenth and sixteenth centuries was organized in several strata.[1] Roughly speaking, monastic schools, village schools and particularly the grammar-schools, catered for instruction corresponding to modern 'elementary' and 'secondary' education. These institutions tend to retain the late mediaeval curriculum, except when enlightened individuals such as John Stanbridge and Robert Whittinton inculcate more progressive ideas. During the vicissitudes suffered by schools during the reigns of Henry VIII and Edward VI there was, however, some opportunity for breaking down the old tradition. Laymen begin to play an increasingly important part in the foundation of schools[2] and many schools which had been under

[1] For detailed examination see:
A. F. Leach, *Educational Charters and Documents* (1911).
English Schools at the Reformation, 1546-1548 (1896).
The Schools of Mediaeval England (1904).
Foster Watson, *The English Grammar Schools to 1660: their curriculum and practice* (1908).
The Old Grammar Schools (1916).
Histories and statutes of particular schools:
e.g., Nicholas Carlisle, *A Concise Description of the endowed Grammar Schools in England and Wales*, 2 vols. (1818).
[2] See Foster Watson, *English Grammar Schools to 1660* (1908), for details and examples.

EDUCATION: TUTOR AND SCHOOLMASTER

ecclesiastical control were transferred to secular jurisdiction. St. Paul's School bulks large in the progress of Early Tudor education because it brought home to Colet's contemporaries the changes which were taking place. The significance of the transference to lay control of so prominent a school must have drawn attention to the place taken by education in the contemporary ferment of ideas. The change was not a new thing, but it was the most important of its kind.[1]

To some extent, changing conceptions are reflected in the text-books of the period and in the comments of the many 'Vulgaria,' English sentences for translation into Latin, some of which sought to sharpen the pupil's interest by touching upon topical matters. The invention of printing helps the progress of new ideas. Robert Whittinton, of the Magdalen College School group of Tudor grammarians, acknowledges the debt of the schools to the invention of printing:

> It concludeth many thynges in shorter space than ye wrytten hande doeth / & more ornately sheweth.[2]
> It hyndreth not so moche ye scryueners / but profeteth moche more poore scholers.[3]

Printing made possible the wider circulation of grammars, so that the influence of the most important schoolmasters was extended. Sir Thomas Elyot, writing in 1531, comments on the increased facilities for learning both the classical languages, for

> ... as touchynge grammere, there is at this day better introductions, and more facile, than euer before was made, concernyng as wel greke as latine, if they be wisely chosen.[4]

The teaching in grammar schools made considerable strides towards a combination of new ideas concerning literature and language with the older standards, wherever

---

[1] See A. F. Leach, 'Colet's Place in the History of Education,' *Journal of Education*, (June 1904), pp. 438-439. 'St. Paul's School before Colet,' *Archaeologia*, Vol. 62, Part I (1910), pp. 191-238.

[2] *Vulgaria* (1520), ed. B. White, E.E.T.S. (Original Series No. 187) 1932, p. 106, ll. 21-22.

[3] *Ibid.*, ll. 26-27.   [4] *Gouernour*, Vol. I, p. 33.

EARLY TUDOR CRITICISM

through enlightened endowment or discriminating personnel directing the teaching, permeation was made possible.

There were many difficulties to be combated. For the few men of insight, there were all those who were poorly equipped even to undertake the ordinary teaching of grammar. There must have been many a grammar school master of the kind described by Elyot, who says that

> now a dayes, if to a bachelar or maister of arte studie of philosophie waxeth tediouse, if he haue a spone full of latine, he wyll shewe forth a hoggesheed without any lernyng, and offre to teache grammer and expoune noble writers, and to be in the roome of a maister: he wyll, for a small salarie, sette a false colour of lernyng on propre wittes, whyche wyll be wasshed away with one shoure of raine.[1]

In Whittinton's *Vulgaria* is an example to the same effect:

> (Discipulus) But we maye se dayly / y^t many take vpon them to teyche / for whome it were more expediente to lerne.[2]

The Magdalen College School group and men of their calibre were working against considerable difficulties, but they were tough enough to find this a stimulus to their efforts.

A second stratum is the instruction of princes and noblemen by scholars and men of letters. This is nearest to the general intellectual world and the most fully developed humanist thought of the period in men such as Sir Thomas Wilson and Sir Thomas Elyot. An educational system like that of the *Gouernour* has its parallels in the manuals which treat of the general culture requisite to the man of affairs in the world at large, such as Castiglione's *Courtier*, translated by Sir Thomas Hoby in 1561. Exchange of ideas within the circle of private education took place readily between individual educationalists who could put their systems into practice, whereas new ideas and theories would be relatively slow in penetrating the curricula of

---
[1] *Gouernour*, Vol. 1, pp. 166–167.   [2] *Op. cit.*, p. 110, ll. 32–33.

EDUCATION: TUTOR AND SCHOOLMASTER

institutions. The great European educationalists were in close touch with one another. Ascham corresponded continually with Sturm in Germany. Vives came to England in 1523 and was attached to the court of Henry VIII, becoming tutor to Princess Mary, for whom he wrote the *De Ratione Studii Puerilis* (1523). Erasmus was a link between the scholars of many European countries. Progress moves apace in this sphere, but, as in the grammar schools, by no means unchallenged. The driving power of the most enlightened of private tutors had to combat the indifference of some of the upper classes, which tended to counteract the enthusiasm of the few. In 1519 Alexander Barclay says that the

> vnderstādyng of latyn . . . at this tyme is almost contēned of gentylmen[1]

Elyot, too, deplores the neglect of learning by young men,

> who in their infancie and childehode were wondred at for their aptness to lerning and prompt speakinge of elegant latine, whiche nowe, beinge men, nat onely haue forgotten their congruite, (as is the commune worde), and unneth can speake one hole sentence in true latine, but, that wars is, hath all lernynge in derision, and in skorne therof wyll, of wantonnesse, speake the most barberously that they can imagine.[2]

Elyot holds out some hope for the success of efforts to correct this state of affairs, and says that

> it is apparent . . . men pursuinge it ernestly with discrete iugement and liberalitie, it wolde sone be amended.[3]

The men most influential as tutors in private education are among those most active in the Universities and the world of ideas generally. Ascham and Wilson are stimulated by their acquaintance with the germinal mind of Sir John Cheke at Cambridge and must be considered for their contributions to thought other than the purely educational. Their insight and linguistic alertness, their wrestling with problems of style and of the future of the English language

[1] Translation of Sallust, *op. cit.*, Preface '*Vnto the right hye and mighty prince: Thomas duke of Northfolke.*'
[2] *Gouernour*, Vol. 1, pp. 115–116.   [3] *Ibid.*, Vol. 1, p. 169.

61

are sometimes too easily generalized to apply to the state of University education during their time. The monastic organization and dialectic method of the Universities, the temporary dislocation caused by the dissolution of the monasteries and strong conservative inertia tend to delay progress. Innovations made in statutes and prescribed curricula indicate the working of a new leaven of ideas, but the enforcing of these regulations and the influence of the personnel are more subtle matters for speculation. Instances of individual awareness of change, of independent or progressive method advised or embodied in textbook or manual, are the outward and visible signs of a changing approach to training in classical studies, of building up of method and awakening of discrimination, but, as regards practical results, allowance must always be made for institutional 'time-lag' and the recalcitrance of human material.

The reigns of Henry VIII and Edward VI were troubled times for the schools. The dissolution of the monasteries caused the abolition, or at least temporary suspension, of many schools and there is a hiatus for a time before other foundations replaced them. The stress laid upon the damage done to educational facilities by the dissolution of the monasteries can be exaggerated. It has been pointed out[1] that the monasteries kept schools mainly for their own choristers and that they contributed little to general education. In cases where schools were under the government of monasteries, the payments for mastership were continued. Although the survival of manuscripts throughout the Dark Ages in Europe was largely due to their preservation in the libraries of monasteries, the monks did little to disseminate this knowledge.[2] The foundation of grammar schools, many of which were under secular control, made learning accessible to a much larger class, creating and cultivating the taste of the average reading public to which

[1] See A. F. Leach, *Schools of Mediaeval England* (1915), p. 310.
[2] See G. Baskerville, *English Monks and the Suppression of the Monasteries* (1937), p. 41.

EDUCATION: TUTOR AND SCHOOLMASTER

so much Early Tudor work was addressed. This change in the organization of education makes for a certain loosening of old ideas, for the adaptation of newer, more liberal conceptions of knowledge to augment the older systems.

Among Tudor schoolmasters were a few men of varied interests whose contacts with other activities of the period gave them a wider outlook. William Horman, master of Eton in 1485, fellow in 1502, vice-provost in 1503, is credited by Bale with many works on a wide range of subjects. Nicholas Udall, who became headmaster of Eton in 1534, is the author of the first English comedy on classical models, *Ralph Roister Doister* (c. 1552) and translator of the work of the Colossus of learning of his age, Erasmus. Richard Sherry, headmaster of Magdalen College School from 1534 to 1540, is the author of rhetorical treatises in English.[1]

With the name of Magdalen College School, is associated the work of John Stanbridge and his pupils, Robert Whittinton and William Lily. John Stanbridge, Informator of the school from 1488–1494, proceeded later to the Mastership of the Hospital of St. John at Banbury and became celebrated for his teaching.[2] The *Day Book of John Dorne* (1520) provides evidence for the wide circulation of his grammatical work. Of his *Accidens* there are twenty-seven mentions and twelve of his *Opuscula*.[3] By the time of Robert Whittinton's *Vulgaria* (printed by Pynson and by Wynkyn de Worde in 1520), the advances of a new spirit in the age are perceptible. Sir Thomas More at the end of 1517 spoke of

> this yong bladed and newe shotte vp corne, which hath alredy begonne to sprynge vp bothe in Latine and Greke learnynge,

from which, he says,

---

[1] *A Treatise of Schemes and Tropes gathered out of the best Grammarians and Oratours ... Whereunto is added a declamation written fyrst in Latin by Erasmus* (1550).
A Treatise of the Figures of Grammer and Rhetorike (1555).
[2] Cf. Foster Watson, *The English Grammar Schools to 1660* (1908), pp. 235–238.
[3] See F. Madan, *Oxford Historical Society Collectanea*, Series I, Part 3, p. 172, col. 2.

I looke for plentiful increase at length of goodly rype grayne. . . .[1]

Whittinton also comments on the recovery of true scholarship:

The excellent inuencyons of men in this dayes shewe that the golden vayne / or golden worlde (by reuolucyon celestyall) is now retourned / or come agayne.[2]

For true knowlege of lernyng that hath longe tym be hydde in profounde derkenes / by dylygence of men in this tyme is nowe brought to open lyght.[3]

and upon the value of such recovered knowledge:

The true knowlege of lernynge is to suche dylygente studentes more treasure / than rynges & cuppes of golde / & other worldly and transitory ryches.[4]

For when all this precyous Jewels of golde / syluer plates / & ryche roobes of purple / veluet / clothe of gold be worne or gone by chaunce. lerning wyl abyde with a man.[5]

Whittinton's words mark the consciousness of a transition to new studies of which the foundations can be laid in the early grammar school training. The authority of the older grammarians is being replaced by a more living study. As Skelton says with his characteristic pungent conciseness:

> *Albertus de modo significandi*,
> And *Donatus* be dryuen out of scole;
> Prisians hed broken now handy dandy,
> And *inter didascalos* is rekened for a fole;
> Alexander, a gander of Menanders pole,
> With *Da Causales*, is cast out of the gate,
> And *Da Racionales* dare not show his pate.
>
> *Plauti* in his comedies a chyld shall now reherse,
> And medyll with Quintylyan in his Declamacyons,
> That Pety Caton can scantly construe a verse,
> With *Aveto in Graeco*, and such solempne salutacyons,

---

[1] 'Thomas More to Peter Giles sendeth gretynge,' prefixed to *Utopia*, 2nd edition. Translation by Ralph Robynson (1551), ed. J. H. Lupton (1895), pp. 5–6.
[2] *Op. cit.*, p. 62, ll. 22–24.   [3] *Ibid.*, ll. 28–30.
[4] *Ibid.*, ll. 35–37.   [5] *Ibid.*, p. 63, ll. 3–5.

EDUCATION: TUTOR AND SCHOOLMASTER

Can skantly the tensis of his coniugacyons;
Settynge theyr myndys so moche of eloquens,
That of theyr scole maters lost is the whole sentens.[1]

The mention of Quintilian is significant, for the renewed study of the *Institutio Oratoria* is one of the most powerful stimuli of a more creative study of the classics. The classical conception of 'grammar' derived from Quintilian included the reading of poets and historians as well as the theory and practice of syntactical usage. During the Middle Ages, this study, which corresponded to that of literature, was obscured by the subtleties of scholastic thought. Logic and dialectic superseded grammar, which became the study of the laws under which thought was held rather than of the science of expression. The older conception is retained by a few individuals such as Servatus Lupus, Bernard of Chartres and John of Salisbury in the twelfth, and Vincent de Beauvais in the thirteenth, centuries. It is noteworthy that these men were acquainted with the genuine, though incomplete, *Institutio Oratoria*, whereas knowledge of the writings of Quintilian was mostly confined during this period to the *Declamationes* ascribed to him.[2] The teaching of Bernard of Chartres corresponds very closely with that of the humanists of the Renascence period. He taught the rules of accidence and syntax side by side with example, training an independent faculty of criticism in his pupils. The account of his methods given by John of Salisbury[3] shows that it contributed to a valuable cultivation of the mind instead of concentrating upon arid linguistic intricacies.

Apart from this manifestation of unusual powers in individuals, the study of ancient literature was neglected in the Middle Ages. 'Not one of the classics of antiquity is prescribed in the statutes of the various Universities of Europe in the thirteenth and fourteenth centuries.'[4] This

---

[1] *Speke Parrot, op. cit.*, Vol. 2, p. 9, ll. 174–187.
[2] See J. E. Sandys, *A Short History of Classical Scholarship* (1915), p. 152.
[3] Quoted H. O. Taylor, *The Mediaeval Mind* (1911), Vol. 2, pp. 130–131.
[4] See L. J. Paetow, *The Arts Course at the Mediaeval Universities* (Illinois University Studies, Vol. 3, No. 7), 1910, for discussion.

EARLY TUDOR CRITICISM

state of affairs continues until, in the fourteenth and early fifteenth centuries in Italy, there is a revival of classical studies and a corresponding impulse towards a recreation of the spirit of *humanitas*, the conversion of knowledge to the shaping and extension of the resources of the human spirit and personality. In 1416 a complete copy of the manuscript of Quintilian's *Institutio Oratoria* was discovered by Poggio at the monastery of St. Gall.[1] From this recovery of a more extensive knowledge of the educational ideals of the ancients dates a new phase of study.

Its influence is reflected in the establishment of schools in Europe on the basis of Quintilian's system. Peter Ramus followed up his dramatic protest against Aristotelianism in his Master's disputation in Paris (1536)[2] with a different mode of teaching in the College of Ave Maria. There he followed the precepts of Quintilian in enforcing the explanation of grammatical precepts with selected examples from the best of classical authors and orators. In Germany, Johan Sturm, on appointment to the Strasburg School in 1538, instituted his ten-year courses of Latin and Greek studies with the same basic principles. Vives in France also adopted from Quintilian the conception of grammar as embracing the study of literature with a broad cultural bearing.[3]

These ideas reach England first through the acquaintance of scholars with European intellectual circles and their effect is noticeable in the systems drawn up by such men for private education. Elyot's *Gouernour* draws freely upon the work of Quintilian and Ascham's *Scholemaster*, though actually produced as late as 1570, is the result of the circulation of ideas before this date during his close association with the Cambridge circle and other men of active minds. They all have in common the desire to reinstate a study of

[1] See Sandys, *op. cit.*, p. 168.
[2] See F. P. Graves, *Peter Ramus and the Educational Reformation of the Sixteenth Century* (1912), p. 26.
[3] See *De Tradendis Disciplinis* (1531), translated by Foster Watson, *Vives: On Education* (1913).
Cf. also W. H. Woodward, *Studies in Education during the Age of the Renaissance* (1906), pp. 180-209.

EDUCATION : TUTOR AND SCHOOLMASTER

ancient literature as *litterae humaniores* in the full sense of the word, contributing to character as well as to the sharpening of intellectual equipment. Only careful and penetrating study, selecting the characteristic value of each author, could extract the full benefit from such reading as was included in the curriculum. Elyot is

> of Quintiliane's opinion, that there is fewe or none aunceint warke that yeldethe nat some frute or commoditie to the diligent reders.[1]

Grammatical precepts are better drawn from excellent practice by the authors of antiquity than studied in the abstract, so that appreciation of authors contributes to the study of the rules which constitute grammar in its technical aspect.

> 'For without doute,' says Ascham, '*Grammatica* it selfe, is sooner and surer learned by examples of good authors, than by the naked rewles of *Grammarians*.'[2]

Erasmus is equally clear concerning the relation of precept and example in the study of classical language and literature. He says:

> I must make my conviction clear that, whilst a knowledge of the rules of accidence and syntax is most necessary to every student, still they should be as few, as simple, and as carefully framed as possible. . . .
>
> For it is not by learning rules that we acquire the power of speaking a language, but by daily intercourse with those accustomed to express themselves with exactness and refinement, and by the copious reading of the best authors.[3]

In teaching grammar on the basis of Quintilian, the teacher is obliged to be a man of taste and judgment both literary and linguistic, with the faculty of appreciating both matter and style in his selected authors. Elyot's definition of the grammarian is wide and inclusive:

[1] *Gouernour*, Vol. I, p. 131.
[2] *The Scholemaster* (1570), ed. W. A. Wright (1904), p. 259. Further references will be to this edition.
[3] W. H. Woodward, *Erasmus: Concerning Education*, pp. 163–164. Cf. Vives, *op. cit.*, pp. 100–106.

EARLY TUDOR CRITICISM

I name hym a gramarien, by the autoritie of Quintilian, that speakyng latine elegantly, can expounde good autours, expressynge the inuention and disposition of the mater, their stile or fourme of eloquence, explicating the figures as well of sentences as wordes, leuyng nothyng, persone, or place, named by the autour, undeclared or hidde from his scholers.[1]

The relation of grammatical precepts and the reading of authors is a question which occupies the minds of private tutors and grammar school masters alike. Knowledge of the Latin language was essential throughout the Middle Ages as the language of scholarship and of the Scriptures and reading of the heathen authors was necessary for practice. Grammar therefore preserved incidentally a certain tradition of classical reading such as we find commented on by Hrabanus Maurus in the ninth century:

> *Grammar* teaches us to understand the old poets and historians, and also to speak and write correctly. Without it we cannot understand the figures and unusual modes of expression in the Holy Scriptures, and consequently cannot grasp the sense of the divine word. . . . Hence, industrious reading of the old healthier poets, and repeated exercise in the art of poetic composition are not to be neglected.[2]

With the Renascence period came the desire to study classical literature for its own sake and for the qualities of mind to be derived from it. The importance of the Latin language, too, was increased, since it had become the *cachet* of the man of affairs and culture as well as of the scholar. It was

> necessary in dealing with law and other difficult matters of State, and also the means of mutual communication between us and strangers and foreigners.[3]

Men of the Renascence period were sensitive to linguistic excellence and insisted not only on thorough mastery of Latin, but of 'pure and elegant Latin.'[4] The language had

[1] *Gouernour*, Vol. 1, pp. 164–165.
[2] Quoted G. A. Plimpton, *The Education of Chaucer* (1935), p. 95.
[3] From the Letters patent granted to William Byngham to found the College of God's House in Cambridge (1439), the first training college for grammar school masters. Quoted A. F. Leach, *The Schools of Mediaeval England* (1915), p. 257.
[4] Sir Thomas Elyot, *Gouernour*, Vol. 1, p. 35.

EDUCATION: TUTOR AND SCHOOLMASTER

suffered by the incorporation of debased forms from colloquial usage on the one hand and by a pedantic tincture from the more narrow-minded scholars on the other. Erasmus finds 'grammarians' in the worst sense

> a kynde of men (doubtlesse) most miserable, most slavelike, & most contemptuous. . . . Adde also hereunto, this kynde of delite they have, as often as any of theim chaunceth in some olde boke to fynde out the name of Anchises mother, or some other latine woorde not commenly used, as Bubsequa, Bovinator, Manticulator, or diggeth up some gobbet of an olde stone graven with Romaine or greke letters somewhat defaced. . . .[1]

Vives writes a treatise against the pseudo-dialecticians, whose jargon was equally detrimental to the purity of Latin, and tries to discover 'The Causes of the Corruptions of the Arts.'[2] Mediaeval Latin had incorporated numerous impure forms and William Horman includes in his *Vulgaria* (1519)[3] warnings against solecisms and barbarisms and devotes the last four chapters to words either to be avoided or to be used with care. Ascham does not agree with the practice of speaking Latin in early years and cites the opinion of

> that excellent learned man, G. Budaeus, in his Greeke Commentaries [where he] sore complaineth, that whan he began to learne the latin tonge, vse of speaking latin at the table, and elsewhere, vnaduisedlie, did bring him to soch an euill choice of wordes, to soch a crooked framing of sentences, that no one thing did hurt or hinder him more, all the daies of his life afterward, both for redinesse in speaking, and also good iudgement in writinge.[4]

The starting point of culture in the Renascence period is, therefore, the practice of speaking

---

[1] *The praise of Folie*, translated by Sir Thomas Chaloner, ed. J. E. Ashbee (1901), pp. 45–46.
[2] *De Causis Corruptarum Artium*, the first part of the *De Tradendis Disciplinis*, sometimes quoted separately under this title.
[3] Reprinted, with an Introduction, by M. R. James, for the Roxburgh Club, 1926. All further references will be to this edition.
[4] *The Scholemaster*, p. 185.

EARLY TUDOR CRITICISM

pure latin, which standeth by rule, authoritie *and* custome.[1] The scholar is to be imbued in his earliest years with the necessity for careful speech and the selection of the finest, purest language. Latin speaking is enforced by school statutes upon the grammar school boy[2] as it is by the precepts of men of letters such as Elyot and Ascham. He became accustomed to the idea of examples such as Stanbridge's in his *Vulgaria*, which point out that

It is a gret help for scollars to speke latyn.[3]

and

It longeth to a scollar to speke latyn.[4]

Similarly Horman says:

A man can scant beleue: how great a let and hyndraunce is wronge and fylthy latten or other speche to yonge childrens wyttis / and in especial in theyr fyrste settynge to scole.[5]

Let yonge children be wel taken hede of: that they lerne no latyn / but clene and fresshe.[6]

There is a concerted attack made by educationalists on slovenly speech and an attempt to inculcate, by continual insistence upon excellence of language, a faculty of linguistic judgment. Horman thinks that this attempt is having noteworthy success:

Laten speche: that was almost loste: is nowe after longe absens recouered and come ageyne.[7]

It is acknowledged that

to speake latin is no lawe, but an obseruacion of excellent menne whose iudgement standeth for reason.[8]

These men have a new perception of the value of linguistic study. It is, of course, valuable as the means of access to treasuries of knowledge in Greek and Latin, but they realize also the value of the mental discipline it

---

[1] Richard Sherry, *A Treatise of the Figures of Grammer and Rhetorike* (1555), fol. v^v.
[2] For list of school statutes requiring Latin speaking see Foster Watson, *English Grammar Schools to 1660* (1908), p. 316.
[3] *Op. cit.*, p. 14, l. 26.   [4] *Ibid.*, p. 16, l. 22.   [5] *Op. cit.*, p. 129.
[6] *Ibid.*, p. 131.   [7] *Ibid.*, p. 122.   [8] Richard Sherry, *op. cit.*, fol. v^v–vi^r.

EDUCATION: TUTOR AND SCHOOLMASTER

imposes. Sharpening of the faculties of discrimination, new sensitiveness of intellectual response, are the results of judicious instruction in classical languages, so that, to men trained in such a tradition

> it shall afterwarde be lasse grefe . . . in a maner, to lerne any thing, where they understande the langage wherein it is written.[1]

Linguistic study alone can have this effect upon the mind and the educationalists of the sixteenth century are agreed upon this point. With Erasmus, they say that

> Language . . . claims the first place in the order of studies. . . .[2]

Differences of opinion occur in the relative importance they assign to the learning of rules and the study of examples from which the necessary rules may be deduced, a decision which involves the whole end and aim of learning a language. Some, like Elyot, thought that too laboured concentration upon the framework of syntax and accidence tended to blunt the fine edge of literary appreciation, wearying the desire for knowledge which alone makes learning effective and creative. Elyot advocates the learning of sufficient grammatical usage to make enjoyable reading possible:

> Grammer beinge but an introduction to the understanding of autors, if it be made to longe or exquisite to the lerner, hit in a maner mortifieth his corage: And by that time he cometh to the most swete and pleasant redinge of olde autours, the sparkes of feruent desire of lernynge is extincte with the burdone of grammer, lyke as a lyttel fyre is sone quenched with a great heape of small stickes.[3]

While Elyot is speaking for private education, Colet similarly emphasizes the value of reading in classical literature in his Latin grammar, and says that

> if any man wyll knowe, and by that knowledge attayne to vnderstande latyn bokes, and to speke & to wryte the clene

[1] Elyot, *Gouernour*, Vol. I, p. 33.
[2] W. H. Woodward, *Erasmus: concerning Education*, Part 2, p. 163.
[3] *Gouernour*, Vol. I, p. 55.

EARLY TUDOR CRITICISM

latyn. Let hym aboue all besyly lerne and rede good latyn auctours of chosen poetes and oratours, and note wysely howe they wrote, and spake, and study alway to folowe them, desiryng none other rules but their examples.[1]

Most emphatically of the opposite opinion is Robert Whittinton. In the epistle *Ad lectorem* prefixed to his *Vulgaria* we find a denunciation of the undue importance given to the reading of authors:

> Neque subticere possum eorum insolentiam / qui authorum imitationem preceptis anteponendam (quod sibi soli sapere videantur) affirmant vt preceptores preposteri. Immo nulla precepta grammaticulis tradenda sed solam authorum imitationem cecucientem amplectandam pugillatice contendunt. At quis non rideat eorum inscitiam? vt clauum clauo traduut / & vorsuram sibi soluunt.[2]

He pursues the same train of thought in the examples set for his scholars:

> Imitacyon of autours without preceptes & rules / is but a longe betynge about the busshe & losse of tyme to a yonge begynner.[3]

> It is a wast labour / yf a carpenter / without compas / rule / / lyne & plummet sholde attende to square tymbre frame and reyre ony buyldynge.[4]

> That teycher setteth the cart before the horse that preferreth imitacyon before preceptes.[5]

He turns the argument used by the other side against their own methods and accuses them of dulling the brain and causing confusion of thought by insisting upon reading before complete knowledge of the language has been acquired. He says of the other method:

[1] *Explicit Colet editio*. Appended to *An introductyon of the partes of spekyng / for chyldren and yonge begynners in to latyn speche*. (Wynkyn de Worde, 1534), sig. D. 6ʳ.
He wrote this treatise, he says, 'not thynkynge that I coude say any thing better than hath be sayd before, but I toke this besynesse hauynge great pleasure to shewe the testymony of my good mynde vnto that schole. In which lytell warke if any newe thynges be of me, it is alonely that I haue put these partes in a more clere ordre, and haue made them a lytell more easy to yonge wyttes, than (me thynketh) they were before.' 'A lytell proheme to the booke' (ed. above, sig. A. 5ᵛ).
[2] p. 33, ll. 16–22. [3] *Ibid.*, p. 35, ll. 12–13.
[4] *Ibid.*, p. 35, ll. 20–22. [5] *Ibid.*, p. 36, ll. 2–3.

EDUCATION: TUTOR AND SCHOOLMASTER

> Tendre wyttes with suche derke ambage be made as dull as a betle.[1]

and

> He that laboureth no thynge holy / but catcheth a patche of euery thynge / is mete t[o] pyke a salet.[2]

Whittinton is strongly opposed to the refutation of the older grammarians implicit in the Quintilian tradition. In the same epistle he says:

> Quippe qui precepta abijcienda & negligenda censuerit: priscos illos et illustrissimos grammaticos / Diomedem. Donatum. Phocam. Honoratum Seruium. Priscianum: & (recentiores ne sileam) Sulpitium, Perottum. & de latine lingue elegantijs meritissimum Laurentium vallensem frustratos labores / & quasi laterem lauisse iudicant. Adeo ut tantorum virorum memoriam extinguere: immo artem ipsam grammatices explodere (quamuis cerete cera digni) videantur.[3]

His conception of the scope of the necessary mental equipment of a scholar of grammar is more restricted than that of the admirers of Quintilian. He insists that

> Preceptes is the chefe and moost expedyent bryngyng vp of a yonge grammaryon.[4]

and consequently the office of the teacher will not be so exacting. Quintilian makes of the study of grammar an interpretative study of literature based on insight into language:

> Primus in eo, qui scribendi legendique adeptus erit facultatem, grammatici est locus.[5]

'Grammatica' adopts the function of 'Rhetorica' in so far as it entails the study of authors as well as the rudiments of language, and the more liberal-minded of the educationalists of the Renascence period attempt to restore this ideal. Elyot says:

[1] *Ibid.*, p. 36, ll. 17-18.   [2] *Ibid.*, p. 37, ll. 28-29.
[3] *Ibid.*, p. 34, ll. 3-10.   [4] *Ibid.*, p. 39, ll. 28-29.
[5] *Institutio Oratoria*, with an English translation by H. E. Butler (1921), Vol. 1, pp. 60-61. All further references will be to this edition.

EARLY TUDOR CRITICISM

Verily there may no man be an excellent poet nor oratour unlasse he haue parte of all other doctrine, specially of noble philosophie. And to say the trouth, no man can apprehende the very delectation that is in the leesson of noble poetes unlasse he have radde very moche and in diuers autours of diuers lernynges.[1]

He follows Quintilian closely in emphasizing the fact that the grammarian

may not be ignorant in philosophie, for many places that be almooste in euerye poete fetched out of the subtile parte of naturall questions. These be well nighe the wordes of Quintilian.[2]

The grammarian is thus constituted the literary critic, the guardian of developing taste, the selector of the best literature. William Horman's description of the trouble taken to make the best selection of authors establishes the status of the schoolmaster in the field of literary criticism. He says:

I bestowed moche labour and study / to gette myne authours to gether.

It coste me more labour to chose and discousse my authors / which were beste.[3]

Study of classical authors in the Renascence is wide and inclusive. Erasmus in the treatise *De Ratione Studii* outlines the rules for literary study. He selects a play of Terence. This entails discussion of comedy as a literary *genre* and of the terms used in definition. Study of the linguistic principles follows, with detailed examination of style and diction, taking into account the aim and effects of literature.[4] Comments upon the value of classical authors made by these tutor-critics are the nearest approach to a body of literary criticism in the Early Tudor period. The variety of tone within them indicates the ways in which these authors were considered most valuable for the purposes of Renascence education. Livy, for instance, is esteemed by Elyot for his

[1] *Gouernour*, Vol. 1, p. 131.
[2] Cf. *Institutio Oratoria*, Vol. 1, p. 131.
[3] *Op. cit.*, p. 133.
[4] Woodward, *op. cit.*, pp. 174–177.

EDUCATION: TUTOR AND SCHOOLMASTER

elegancie of writinge, which floweth in him like a fountaine of swete milke,[1] as much as for the instructive purpose of his work. The power to teach and to delight at the same time is to be found in Plato and Cicero.

'Lorde god,' says Elyot, 'what incomparable swetnesse of wordes and mater shall he finde in the saide warkes of Plato and Cicero; wherin is ioyned grauitie with delectation, excellent wysedome with diuine eloquence, absolute vertue with pleasure incredible, and every place is so infarced with profitable counsaile, ioyned with honestie, that those thre bookes be almost sufficient to make a perfecte and excellent gouernour.[2]

The men of this period endeavour to take the long view of classical literature, to assess the value of each author within his setting and in comparison with other work of the same or different languages. Particularly they extend their critical method to the comparison of Latin and Greek, deriving added appreciation of both literatures from the process. Elyot, quick to see the possibilities of the critical activity, sets the epic poets of Greece and Rome together. Virgil, he says,

in his warke called Eneidos, is most lyke to Homere, and all moste the same as Homere, in Latine. Also, by the ioynynge together of these autours, the one shall be the better understande by the other.[3]

The comparison was traditional, but Elyot's recognition of critical process and benefit strengthens the impression of his keenness of perception.

The range of authors recommended for both private and public education represents a wide choice of good literature. The private educationalists organize their reading more directly upon the basis advocated by Quintilian.[4] Erasmus includes among Latin authors Terence, Plautus, Virgil,

---
[1] *Gouernour*, Vol. 1, p. 82.   [2] *Ibid.*, pp. 93-94.
[3] *Ibid.*, p. 61.
Cf. Quintilian: 'ideoque optime institutum est, ut ab Homero atque Vergilio lectio inciperet,' *op. cit.*, Vol. 1, p. 148.
[4] *Ibid.*, Vol. 4, pp. 2-74.

EARLY TUDOR CRITICISM

Horace, Cicero, Caesar and Sallust[1] and of Greek literature Lucian, Demosthenes, Herodotus, Homer, Euripides. Elyot's survey is similar, including Aesop, Lucian, Homer,

> from whom as from a fountaine proceded all eloquence and lernyng,[2]

Virgil, Horace, Lucian, Hesiod. The poets are to be the pupil's chief reading until he is fourteen years of age, after which time the rhetoricians, Cicero, Hermogenes, Quintilian, Isocrates and Demosthenes are to be introduced to him as part of his training for public life. For grammar school reading Wolsey recommends the first class to begin with Horace and to proceed thence through the work of Cato, Aesop, Terence and Virgil who is

> omnium poetarum principem vobis dari, cuius maiestatem carminis voce bene sonore offerendam esse,[3]

then selected epistles of Cicero, with Sallust, Caesar, Horace's *Epistolae* and Ovid's *Metamorphoses* as reading for the higher forms. Since the teaching of Latin is continuous throughout the Middle Ages, the importance of Renascence teaching lies in its changed emphasis, the desire to extract the greatest possible value out of classical authors. It should provide critical standards and stimulate the creative power. Whittinton says acutely:

> I se many of them in this dayes yt taketh vpon them to dysprayse other me*n*nes workes / but I se fewe or none of them y setteth out ony of theyr owne makynge.[4]

> Yf ony of theym wyll take vpon them the iudgemente or correccyon of other men: fyrst it wold become them to lerne to make of theyr owne inuencyon.[5]

Greek scholarship had not a tradition similar to that of Latin before the Renascence period and the appearance of instruction in this language in public schools and in systems of private tutors marks a step towards a wider survey of

---

[1] *See* Woodward, *op. cit.*, p. 12. [2] *Gouernour*, Vol. 1, p. 58.
[3] *Rudimenta Grammatices* (1529), 'Quartae Classis.' [4] *Op. cit.*, p. 71, ll. 3–5.
[5] *Ibid.*, ll. 21–23.

EDUCATION : TUTOR AND SCHOOLMASTER

classical knowledge and a new interest in linguistic study to be derived from the juxtaposition of Greek and Latin.

Erasmus in his work *De Ratione Studii* insists upon the simultaneous study of both languages because

> within these two literatures are contained all the knowledge, which we recognize as of vital importance to mankind.

He thinks too,

> that the natural affinity of the two tongues renders it more profitable to study them side by side than apart.[1]

Elyot, with his faithful adherence to the authority of Quintilian for instructing his pupil,

> wolde haue hym lerne greke and latine autors both at one time: orels to begyn with greke, for as moche as that it is hardest to come by: . . . And if a child do begyn therin at seuen yeres of age, he may continually lerne greke autours thre yeres, and in the meane tyme use the Latin tonge as a familiar langage.[2]

Infiltration into the régime of grammar schools is necessarily slower, but the teaching of Greek made rapid strides there during the sixteenth century. It is notable that one of the best known of Tudor schoolmasters, William Lily, should be also one of the finest Greek scholars in England in the first quarter of the sixteenth century and that in the Statutes of St. Paul's School, where he became High Master in 1512, he should require any future High Master to be

> a man hoole in body . . . lerned in good and cleane Latin literature, and also in Greke, yf such may be gotten.[3]

By the mid-sixteenth century, Greek teaching seems to have been firmly established in the schools. Sir Thomas Pope, writing of his school days at Eton, says that

> the Greek tongue was growing apace.[4]

and some of Horman's examples in his *Vulgaria* refer to this study:

---

[1] Translated Woodward, *op. cit.*, Part 2, p. 163.   [2] *Gouernour*, Vol. 1, p. 54.
[3] *The Statutes of St. Paul's School* (1512), from the reprint of 1816, by one of the Trustees, p. 4, *Capitulum primum de Magistro primario*. Sig. A. 2ᵛ.
[4] Quoted Foster Watson, *op. cit.*, p. 495.

EARLY TUDOR CRITICISM

We haue played a comedi of greke.[1]

I shall rede openly a lectur of greke / if so be / that honest wagis be assigned out for the yere.[2]

and a comment on the schoolboy who

applied hym self with great diligence to greke.[3]

The identification of knowledge of Greek with new and progressive ideas is proved by the opposition with which it met in University circles, where its incursion is felt more rapidly and more strongly than elsewhere. Progress depended upon the success of a few individuals against a strongly resisting body of conservatism. Erasmus lectured in Greek at Cambridge in 1511, but the duration of his visit was not long enough to establish the study securely. This was only secured by the time Richard Cooke of King's College was appointed Greek Reader at Cambridge, in 1519.

With the generation of Cheke and his associates at Cambridge in the mid-sixteenth century the new ideas make rapid progress and the study of Greek language and literature is successfully promulgated by them. Ascham writes to Brondesby in 1542:

> ARISTOTELES nunc et PLATO, quod factum est etiam apud nos hoc quinquennium, in sua lingua a pueris leguntur. SOPHOCLES et EURIPIDES sunt hic familiarores, quam olim PLAUTUS fuerit quum tu hic eras. HERODOTUS, THUCYDIDES, XENOPHON, magis in ore et manibus teruntur, quam TITUS LIVIUS. Quod de CICERONE olim, nunc de DEMOSTHENE audires. Plures ISOCRATES hic in manibus puerorum habentur, quam tum TERENTII. Nec Latinos interim aspernamur, sed optimos quosque et seculo illo aureo florentes ardentissime amplexamur.[4]

The name of Sir John Cheke again appears as the driving force and Ascham gives his far-sighted choice of literature and enthusiasm as a teacher as the reason for the swift response to Greek studies:

> Hunc literarum ardorem et incendit et fovit CHECI nostri

[1] *Op. cit.*, p. 131. [2] *Ibid.*, p. 135. [3] *Ibid.*, p. 137.
[4] *Works*, ed. Giles (1865), Vol. I, Part 1, p. 26.

EDUCATION: TUTOR AND SCHOOLMASTER

labor et exemplum. Qui publice gratis praelegit totum HOMERUM, totum SOPHOCLEM, et id bis: totum EURIPIDEM, omnem fere HERODOTUM. Id quod fecisset in omnibus Graecis poetis, historiographis, oratoribus, philosophis, nisi pessimum fatum tam felicem literarum progressum nobis invidisset.[1]

The checking of this impulse to acquire a more extensive and more liberal knowledge of classical literature by Stephen Gardiner[2] and his supporters shows how firm was the bedrock of tradition against which any novelty or broadening activity of the mind had to be asserted. In spite of this, the recurrence of the names of the Cambridge Circle, associated with views showing insight and critical perception, point to a period in the mid-sixteenth century when the teaching of classical language and literature was definitely humanist in colouring. The recovery of the Greek ideal of culture was by no means complete everywhere, but these men made a valuable attempt to see literature and language steadily and to see them whole.

Admission of the vernacular as the language for the actual teaching of Latin was only reluctantly allowed by men to whom Latin was the scholarly language. Erasmus would not allow the use of the vernacular after the early stages of education, when it might be used for setting the subject for composition. Vives has the credit of advancing a claim for the mother tongue of the scholar in *De Tradendis Disciplinis* possibly deriving his opinion from the Spaniard, Antonio de Nebrija.[3] In France, Mathurin Cordier writing *De Corrupti Sermonis Emendatione Libellus* (1536), takes French as the medium of Latin teaching. This advocacy of the vernacular in the exclusive educational field is a definite increase of prestige. John Palsgrave, tutor to Princess Mary, states[4] the vital condition of education, the complete fusion

---
[1] *Ibid.*
[2] His *Edicta De Pronuntiatione linguae Latinae et Graecae* were issued in 1542.
[3] See Palsgrave's *Acolastus*, ed. P. L. Carver, E.E.T.S. (Original Series, No. 202, 1937), Introduction, p. xci, Note 4.
[4] *Ibid.*, Introduction, pp. xi–xii.

EARLY TUDOR CRITICISM

between thought and expression in the minds of both teacher and pupil. The process of thought in the native tongue must therefore be quite clear before the meaning can be adequately expressed in any other language. Palsgrave deplores the wide-spread neglect of the vernacular by the learned, who thus impair their ability to examine Latin and English side by side accurately or productively:

> And somme other furthermore there be, whiche thoughe they haue by their greatte studye, . . . soo moche prouffyted in the Latyne tongue, that to shewe an euydente tryalle of theyr lernynge, they canne wryte an Epistle ryght latyne lyke, and therto speake latyne, as the tyme shall mynyster // occasyon, very well . . . yet for all this, partely bycause of the rude language vsed in their natyue countreyes, where they were borne and firste lerned (as it happened) their grammer rules, & partely bycause that commyng streyght from thense . . . they haue not had occasions to be conuersaunte in suche places of your realme, as the pureste englysshe is spoken, they be not able to expresse theyr conceyte in theyr vulgar tonge, ne be not suffycyente, perfectly to open the diuersities of phrases betwene our tonge and the latyn (whiche in my poore iudgement is the veray chiefe thynge that the schole mayster shulde trauayle in).[1]

In the early stages of education, too much learning can be a dangerous thing for reasons which Palsgrave very acutely gives. He deplores the practice of those teachers, who,

> hauyng no due consyderation to the tender wyttes, whiche they take vnder theyr charge to teache in the stede of pure englyshe wordes and phrases, . . . declare to their chylderne one latyne worde by an nother, and confounde the phrases of the tongues: And thus not a lytell do hynder their yong scholers, while they wold seme for their own partes to haue a knowledge and erudition aboue the common sort.[2]

Elyot is of the same opinion and advocates for the pupil a preliminary clear understanding of grammar by means of vernacular teaching before proceeding to more advanced work:

[1] *Op. cit.*, 'Epystle to the Kynges Hyghnes,' p. 5, l. 32–p. 6, l. 13.
[2] *Ibid.*, p. 5, ll. 2–9.

EDUCATION: TUDOR AND SCHOOLMASTER

> After that the childe hathe ben pleasantly trained, and induced to knowe the partes of speche, and can seperate one of them from an other, in his owne langage, it shall than be time that his tutor or gouernour do make diligent serche for suche a maister as is excellently lerned both in greke and latine. . . .[1]

Admission to the grammar school of the Tudor period presupposed a certain knowledge of English. Dean Colet, introducing his *Aeditio*, which he wrote for St. Paul's School (1534), says:

> If your chylde can rede, and wryte latyn and Englysshe suffycyently, so that he be able to rede & wryte his owne lesons, thā he shall be admytted in to the schole for a scholer.[2]

Horman, among the examples in his *Vulgaria*, includes a tribute to the masters of the vernacular in Italy as well as in England for their achievement in imaginative literature:

> Dantes Patrarcke / Boccasse / Chaucer / Gowar and Lydgate were goodly makers of feyned narrations.[3]

This care for the vernacular should neutralize the bias towards classical knowledge exclusive of achievement in the vulgar tongue, which Grimald comments upon in those 'clerks' who

> could conceiue, & vnderstande full well: whose toung neuerthelesse in vtterauce, and vse of speache, was in a maner maymed: yea and some, that could also speake latine reddily, and wel fauoredly: who to haue done as much in our language, & to haue handled the same matter, wold haue bin half blāk. what nede mo words?[4]

Sir Thomas More is an advocate of instruction in the vernacular and his stress upon this method for the citizens of Utopia and admiration for the qualities of their language, throw light upon his hopes for the English language. He says:

> They be taughte learninge in theire owne natyue tonge. For yt is bothe copious in woordes and also pleasaunte to the eare, and for the vtteraunce of a mans minde verye perfecte and sure.[5]

[1] *Gouernour*, Vol. I, p. 50.   [2] sig. A. iv.   [3] *Op. cit.*, p. 134.
[4] Translation of Cicero, *op. cit.*, Preface.   [5] *Utopia, op. cit.*, pp. 183–184.

EARLY TUDOR CRITICISM

The vernacular has, therefore, champions in the educational world fit to take their place with the translators and with men like Sir Thomas Wilson in academic circles. Such a one is Palsgrave. He shares his advocacy of the vernacular with Vives, but he carries his convictions a stage farther. Whereas Vives has always in mind the ultimate improvement of Latin, Palsgrave considers the other side as well. He does not discount the incidental benefits derived by the vernacular or make it subordinate to the other aim. He looks forward to

> suche an establyshed mariage, betwene the two tonges, as may be vnto such of your graces subiectes, as shall succede hereafter, not only stedy, agreed vpon, and parmanent, but also an incredible furtheraunce, to atteyn the pure latinitie by.[1]

Like Sir Thomas Wilson, he envisages the establishment of a standard English speech. He thinks that

> if this kynde of interpretation maye take effecte, and be put in execution, not onely the speache of your subiectes shoulde by that meane haue a great aduantage to waxe vniforme, throughe out all your graces domynions, but also the englysshe tonge, which vnder your graces prosperouse reygne is comme to the hygheste perfection that euer hytherto it was, shulde by this occasion remayne more stedy and parmanent in his endurance, not onely by the well kepynge of his perfection alredy obteyned but also haue a great occasion to come to his most hyghest estate, and there, by that meanes longe to be preserued.[2]

His sincere belief in the potentialities of the English language impels him to make a translation of a work which was accomplished by Fullonius

> through the dylygent obseruation of the pure latyn authors.[3]

That there was a keen demand for such translations is recognized by Robert Whittinton, who is a translator as well as a schoolmaster. He says of his translation of Cicero's *De Officiis*:

> The fynall cause wherfore I toke in hande this noble monu-

---
[1] *Op. cit.*, 'Epystle to the Kynges Hyghnes,' p. 9, ll. 28-32.
[2] *Ibid.*, p. 10, ll. 6-17.   [3] *Ibid.*, p. 9, ll. 8-9.

EDUCATION: TUTOR AND SCHOOLMASTER

ment to be translate in to my natyue and englysshe tonge is this: I se many yonge persones / and rather all for the most parte that be any thyng lettred / of whome some scantly can skyll of letters / very studyous of knowlege of thynges / and be vehemently bente to rede newe workes / and in especyall that be translated in to the vulgare tonge. All be it some of theym where as they iudge them selfe very fruytfully exercysed / not withstandyng they seme vaynly occupyed / and they perceyue very lytell fruyte to issue out of their studye.[1]

The names of Whittinton and Horman are joined in the undignified 'Antibossicon' controversy. The outcome of Horman's Mastership at Eton from 1485-1494 was the 'Vulgaria' published in 1519 for the use of Eton boys. Whittinton's 'Vulgaria' was issued in 1520 and this precipitated the ignoble quarrel in which Skelton took part.[2] Among their differences of opinion was that of the emphasis to be laid upon linguistic precept or literature in grammatical training. Whittinton, staunch upholder of the linguistic point of view, is strong in defence of the vernacular:

> Syth euery countre doeth auaunse with laude his owne language whye sholde not we thynke worthy our language the same? sythen al speeches suffre confusyon saue hebrewe.[3]

By the time of Whittinton, the spirit of emulation which spurred on the translators and all men of letters who had the welfare of the vernacular at heart had quickened this interest and attention to the qualities of the English language was becoming a serious literary duty. The mental discipline and judgment acquired by classical reading planned in the most liberal tradition is applied equally to the vernacular. Ascham formulates this attitude with the admonition that

> in euerie separate kinde of learning and studie, by it selfe, ye must follow, choiselie a few, and chieflie some one, and that namelie in our schole of eloquence, either for penne or talke.... //

[1] *The thre bookes of Tullyes offyces / bothe in latyne tonge & in englysshe* (1534), sig. b. 3ʳ.
[2] John Bale credits him with *Carmen inuectiuum in Guilhelmum Lilium poetam laureatum. lib.* 1. Autograph Note-book, p. 253. (See B. White, *op. cit.*, Introduction, p. xix.)
[3] *op. cit.*, p. 94, ll. 12-14.

EARLY TUDOR CRITICISM

And this not onelie to serue in the *Latin* or *Greke* tong, but also in our own English language. But yet, bicause the prouidence of God hath left vnto vs in no other tong, saue onelie in the *Greke* and *Latin* tong, the trew preceptes, and perfite examples of eloquence, therefore must we seeke in the Authors onelie of those two tonges, the trewe Paterne of Eloquence, if in any other mother tongue we looke to attaine, either to perfit vtterance of it our selues, or skilfull iudgement of it in others.[1]

This passage is remarkably comprehensive in its scope. It crystallizes the relations between the classical languages and the vernaculars, makes specific application of the stylistic rules of rhetoric to the written as well as to the spoken work and points out the exercise of the critical faculty to be observed in creation as well as in judgment of the work of others.

In the sphere of education as in so many other literary and linguistic discussions, rhetoric exerts strong influence, since it focusses attention on style and arrangement. Horman comments on the popularity of the study of rhetoric in the Tudor period:

> Eloquens is moste allowed and made of amonge al other science of the people.[2]

and Richard Sherry writes his *Treatise of the Figures of Grammar and Rhetorike* for those who are

> studious of Eloquence, and in especiall for suche as in Grammer scholes doe reade moste eloquente Poetes, and Oratours.[3]

Sherry stresses the importance of the study of grammar as training the sense of appropriateness of words for matter, which is the *elocutio* of the rhetorician. The quality of clarity and exactness is a result of grammatical training:

> The plain & euident speache is learned of Grammarians, and it kepeth the oratiō pure, and without al fault: and maketh that every thyng may seme to be spoke, purely, apertly, & clerely.[4]

The grammarians aim at the style described by Quintilian as 'emendata, dilucida, ornata'[5] and controlled by reason,

[1] *Scholemaster*, pp. 282–283.   [2] *Op. cit.*, p. 122.   [3] Colophon.
[4] *Ibid.*, Sig. Aiii^v.   [5] *Op. cit.*, Vol. 1, p. 113.

EDUCATION: TUTOR AND SCHOOLMASTER
tradition and usage:
> Sermo constat ratione vel vetustate, auctoritate, consuetudine.[1]

Comments on style in the *Vulgaria* of William Horman indicate the main trends of contemporary linguistic fashion and conviction. Like Sir Thomas Wilson, he advises avoidance of the obscurely ornate which was so popular:
> Thy maner of wryttynge is darke: with ouer moche curiosite.[2]
> This maner of writynge is to exquysite / and to moche labourde: and so is darke and vnsauery.[3]
> The olde men dyd nat set by the smothe an florysshed style / the whiche is nowe moche made of.[4]

He prefers 'a playn and a clenly maner of wryttyng.'[5]

He mentions archaisms, to be used only judiciously and appropriately:
> Wordis of ferne yeres / so that they be not to olde / and out of knowlege / nor stud(i)ed for a purpose / nor to ofte brought forthe: make the langage substanciall and plesaunt.[6]

The rule for the choice of words with a flavour of antiquity is Quintilian's golden mean between new coinages and archaic revivals:
> Of newe wordis the oldest be beste: and the neweste of the olde.[7]

Educational rules and practice and the fertile open minds of the best of the men associated with education in its various spheres make a valuable contribution to the training of judgment and perception. In the early stages the Tudor schoolboy could be brought up with the views of the most progressive grammarians. Horman, Whittinton, Stanbridge and the rest, whatever their differences on points of detail may be, each have insight into, and conviction of, the

---
[1] *Ibid.*, Vol. 1, p. 112.   [2] *Op. cit.*, p. 132, l. 17.   [3] *Ibid.*, p. 135, ll. 30-31.
[4] *Ibid.*, p. 136, ll. 9-10.   [5] *Ibid.*   [6] *Ibid.*, p. 144, ll. 26-28.
[7] *Ibid.*, p. 144, l. 32.
Cf. Quintilian: 'Cum sint autem verba propria, ficta, translata, propriis dignitatem dant antiquitas. Namque et sanctiorem et magis admirabilem faciunt orationem, quibus non quilibet fuerit usurus. . . .'
Op. cit., Vol. 3, p. 224.

EARLY TUDOR CRITICISM

importance of careful training in classical literature and language with an accompanying regard for the mother tongue. The son of the nobleman is even more directly in the line of new developments in education, when educationalists such as Elyot and Ascham bring to bear the results of their reading of Quintilian and the best of antique authors upon their systems of instruction. Through these men private education is in touch with some of the finest minds of the age. The teaching of Cheke at the University of Cambridge stabilizes the beginnings of critical discrimination which may have been already fostered at an earlier stage of education. The best of educational thought in the Tudor period is quick to realize the possibilities of the faculty of thought and spares no pains to train and develop it to the full. Vives perceives the principle which is the basis of educational ideals:

> But I only call that knowledge which we receive when the senses are properly brought to observe things and in a methodical way to which clear reason leads us on. . . . For art is the means of attaining a sure and predetermined end.[1]

and this may be said to epitomize the aspirations of Tudor education at its most perceptive.

[1] *Op. cit.*, p. 22.

CHAPTER V

THE UNIVERSITIES OF THE EARLY TUDOR PERIOD, WITH SPECIAL REFERENCE TO SIR JOHN CHEKE AND THE CAMBRIDGE CIRCLE

A FOCUS of linguistic criticism and debate in the first half of the sixteenth century lies in another form of the rivalry between Latin and the vernacular. In Europe, where the Romance languages are closely allied to Latin, the literary establishment of the vernacular may be said to have been accomplished during the Middle Ages. In England the position was rather different. Rapid progress had been made during the Anglo-Saxon period, elsewhere for vernaculars a 'dark age,' but from the time of the Norman Conquest until the fourteenth and fifteenth centuries the English language had to contend with French domination. After this time it was re-established as the national language and was justified by considerable literary achievement. Latin was, however, still the language of scholarship and the appreciation of the excellence of classical Latin, which was a result of the sixteenth-century revival of learning in Europe, was an advertisement of its claims.

Pure Latinity was equated with rigorous and exclusive reproduction of the style of Cicero by Pietro Bembo in Italy[1] and Etienne Dolet in France[2] among the most notable European scholars. The apparatus of stylistic and philological criticism tended to become through their efforts merely a means to restricted imitation of their selected master. This vexed question of 'imitation' is itself a controversy which discussed many problems of language and clarified the method of approach to the literature of antiquity. Scholars were agreed that approximation to classical standards of excellence was the best means of reaching

[1] *Ep. Fam.* v. 17. Quoted Woodward, *op. cit.*, p. 54.
[2] *De Imitatione Ciceroniana adversus Erasmam Rot. pro C. Longolio* (1535).

EARLY TUDOR CRITICISM

similar standards in contemporary work. They were divided on the question of how far this excellence could be reproduced in the terms of the originals, or adapted for individual talent and for the requirements of a different age. The Ciceronians argued that the usefulness of the vernaculars was limited to their several countries, that they were still fluid and amorphous by reason of dialectal variation and therefore quite unfit for serious literary purposes. Only by writing in Latin could writers of the Renascence period claim a place with their masters and thus merit equally lasting fame. The choice of Cicero for imitation is itself an act of criticism, but one which could not be at the same time creative, because it defeated its own ends. It was a tacit admission by its partisans that Latin was a dead language, incapable of receiving new life from the present, and effective only if revived in its antique integrity. A more creative study of the classics is that which recognizes the importance of individuality, as maintained by Pico in his discussion with Bembo[1] and by Erasmus.[2] They realized that Ciceronianism could never be more than an academic preoccupation, as compared with the fusion of critical training and individual creative effort. Theirs is a recognition of the spirit of language instead of a pedantic attention to the letter. This controversy involved more than the question of the relative value of Latin and the vernacular. It provided opportunities for the display of fundamental differences of mental habit and critical approach.

The study of any author imposes the use of definite critical standards to know

> which way to folow that one: in what place: by what meane and order: by what tooles and instrumentes ye shall do it, by what skill and iudgement, ye shall trewelie discerne, whether ye folow rightlie or no.[3]

The discipline of imitation as described by Ascham entails

[1] *Ad P. Bembum, de imitatione* (1530, written 1512).
[2] See W. H. Woodward, *op. cit.*, p. 57.
[3] Ascham, *Scholemaster, op. cit.*, pp. 266–267.

THE UNIVERSITIES

wide and sensitive reading, discriminating judgment,[1] collation and comparison,[2] with stress upon the importance of example as well as of precept:

> For preceptes in all Authors, . . . without applying vnto them, the Imitation of examples, be hard, drie, and cold, and therfore barrayn, vnfruitfull and vnpleasant.[3]

With the stimulating help of

> the cunningest Master, and one of the worthiest Ientlemen that ever England bred, *Syr Iohn Cheke*. . . .[4]

and that of his friend Sturm, Ascham outlines a liberal study of both language and literature and this is regarded as not only the necessary preparation for reproduction in English, but also as the ground of criticism or 'skilfull iudgement'.[5] The course of this controversy was further complicated by the necessity of admitting the increasing importance of the vernaculars. The countries of Europe were determined to develop their own resources. Political necessity gave strong support to the establishment of a national language, but the writer who used his mother tongue, had, even so, to justify his choice and there was always, therefore, the opportunity to strengthen the stock defences by some new conviction. Italy had faced the problems in the fourteenth and fifteenth centuries when discussions such as Dante's *Convivio* and *De Vulgari Eloquentia* had been supplemented by his use of the vernacular for the *Divina Commedia*. By the sixteenth century the effects of the Revival of Learning were apparent in France. The place of the vernacular as a literary language was hotly debated in the circle of writers round Du Bellay and by Rabelais and Amyot among others.

Linguistic criticism was therefore a habit of European

---

[1] '. . . so would I haue our scholer alwayes able to do well by order of learnyng and right skill of iudgement.' *Ibid.*, p. 270.
[2] 'Would to God, I might once see, some worthie student of *Aristotle* and *Plato* in Cambridge, that would ioyne in one booke the preceptes of the one with the examples of the other.' *Ibid.*, p. 278.
[3] *Ibid.*, p. 277.   [4] *Ibid.*, p. 268.   [5] *Ibid.*, p. 283.

thought in the sixteenth century. The attention of scholars was fixed on the tempering of their language by preliminary study and imitation of the classics. Poets and men of letters discuss the possibilities of the vernacular, examine it by the newly recovered standards, experiment and test their conclusions. It is an age of eager commerce of ideas, when there is a strong compulsion to debate, to argue and to justify. In the consequent marshalling of ideas defensive and dissenting there are conditions propitious for the evolution of criticism.

English scholars did not become so deeply involved in the Ciceronian controversy as those of Italy and France. They had not the same zest for pure scholarship as the men of Italy in the very heart of the Revival of Learning, nor the desire to draw up rules for a dictatorship of letters which is manifest in France. This is not to say that England was out of touch with the mainstream of culture on the Continent. There was a tradition of humane scholarship already in the group of scholars associated with Humphrey, Duke of Gloucester, in the fifteenth century, and when Erasmus came to England in 1499, More, Linacre, Colet and their circle won his admiration.[1] Even allowing for the hyperbole which characterizes much of the mutual praise of the scholars of this time, this is a genuine tribute to their learning and to the 'civilized' personality accompanying it. An intellectual outlook of this nature would not be confined to sterile and pedantic study of the classics, but would, on the contrary, bring to bear upon them wide and balanced judgment. Praise from the most cosmopolitan scholar of the time shows that England's prestige in the world of letters was considerable.

[1] *Erasmus Roberto Piscatori Agenti in Italia. Anglo. S.D.*: 'textum autem humanitatis atque eruditionis, non illius protritae ac trivialis, sed reconditae, exactae, antiquae, Latinae Graecaeque, ut iam Italiam nisi visendi gratia haud multum desiderem. Coletum meum cum audio, Platonem ipsum mihi videor audire. In Grocino quis illum absolutum disciplinarum orbem non miretur? Linacri iudicio quid acutius, quid altius, quid emunctius? Thomae Mori ingenio quid unquam finxit natura vel mollius vel dulcius vel felicius? ... Mirum est dictu quam hic passim, quam dense veterum litterarum seges efflorescat....'
Selections from Erasmus, P. S. Allen (1908), pp. 31-32.

THE UNIVERSITIES

Scholarship in England is centred in the activity of individuals and of small groups rather than in a continuous tradition. Following the early efflorescence in More and his friends, a man of similar intellectual persuasion is Thomas Lupset, who is a link between them and the Cambridge circle in the middle of the century. The cultivation of judgment and the desire to select the finest work by means of thorough study and clear apprehension are the contributions of scholarship to the formation of criticism. They are clearly active in Lupset, who points the way to the more liberal attitude towards the classics which is the mark of men such as Elyot and Ascham. The manner of his study is essentially a critical one. He realizes that it is not 'the reding of many bokes, that getteth increace of knowledge and iugement...' but a disciplined selection of the best:

> No man ... can vse redinge but in verye fewe workes, the whiche I wolde shuld be piked out of the best sorte, that the fruite of the reders diligence maye be the greatter. I se many lose theyr tyme, when they thinke to bestowe their time beste, bicause they lack iudgemente or knowelege to pyke oute the bokes, the whiche be worthye to be studied.[1]

The coupling of 'iugement' and 'knowelege' is the mark of the scholarship which disintegrates the mass of accumulated information and arranges it according to a considered plan, for

> in euerye thynge an order wel obserued, bringeth more profitte then any laboure or peine besyde.[2]

The germinal centre of mid-sixteenth-century scholarship in England is the group of scholars associated with Sir John Cheke at Cambridge. The influence of Cheke upon his fellows and upon his students is incalculable. He lives rather in the mental outlook of others than in his published work, which is by no means fully representative of his own calibre. The frequent tributes to him are addressed to the stimulus of his personality as much as to his scholarly attainments.

[1] *An Exhortacion to Young Men* (1535 edition). *Life and Works*, ed. J. A. Gee (Yale University Press, 1928), p. 237.
[2] *Ibid.*

EARLY TUDOR CRITICISM

Cambridge in his day must have been a centre of discussion, of controversy upon a basis of wide and liberal culture. Cheke's well-attested contribution to the formation of habits of appreciation and discrimination plays a very important part in the evolution of Tudor criticism.

Some indication of the scope of the interests of the Cambridge circle may be deduced from the extant catalogue of Sir Thomas Smith's Library[1] as representative of their tastes. Pre-occupation with the past did not blind them to the progress of later ages down to their own day. Italian literature in its various phases since the fourteenth century is represented by Dante, Petrarch, Boccaccio and Piccolomini's *D'Institutione d'huomo Nato*. Contemporary linguistic problems in France are represented by Du Bellay's *Defense et Illustration de la langue françoyse* and Jacques Pelcher's *De Pronuntiatione Linguae Gallicae* is there too. This evidence of interest in language is supplemented by Erasmus' *De Copia Verborum* and *De Pronuntiatione* and Smith's knowledge of Hebrew is represented by *Erotemata Linguae Hebraicae*. He possessed also the works of Peter Ramus, whom he had met in Paris, and who made a firm stand against the pre-occupation of learning with Aristotelian logic and scholasticism. This catalogue is at least a pointer to the mental alertness and interests of these men. Stimulating lectures and private discussions made of St. John's College in the mid-sixteenth century a 'little Academe,' in which the personality of Cheke made his teaching effective and creative. The men who absorbed it moved in many spheres of Tudor activity. They were statesmen, educationalists, translators, tutors to the Royal Family and to the aristocracy, friends of the moving spirits of the time in Europe and eager intermediaries with the Continent. Behind them all was the dynamic power of Cheke. Sir Thomas Wilson, among the first to formulate critical principles in the form of a treatise,[2] praises his

[1] Appended to *Life of Sir Thomas Smith*, J. Strype (edition of 1820), pp. 274-281.
[2] *Arte of Rhetorique*, published 1553, corrected and completed 1560, reprinted 1562, 1563, 1567.

> manifolde great gifts and wonderfull vertues: ... his most gentle nature and godly disposed minde, to helpe all those with his knowledge and vnderstanding, that any waye made meanes vnto him, and sought his favour.[1]

Ascham was of the inner circle of Cheke's friends and refers frequently to the private readings and discussions he accorded to them. They derived

> great cōmoditie ... in hearyng hym reade priuatly in his chambre, all Homer, Sophocles, and Euripides, Herodotus, Thucydides, Xenophon, Isocrates and Plato....[2]

The method of study employed in these readings was a systematic testing of chosen examples in the light of critical precepts. The contemporary problem of 'imitation,' mentioned above in connection with the Ciceronian controversy, acquired new meaning in Cheke's study and became a means of approach to the spirit of classical literature rather than an avid reproduction of style alone. Theory and practice were considered together. He is said by Ascham to have made an innovation at Cambridge by the use of this method:

> Cambridge, at my first comming thither, but not at my going away, committed this fault in reading the preceptes of *Aristotle*, without the examples of other Authors.[3]

These men insist upon reasonable application of the rules themselves,

> rather makyng Art by witte, than confoundyng witte by Arte. ... For what mattereth whether we folowe our Booke, or no, if wee folowe witte, and appoint our selfe an order, suche as may declare the truthe more plainely?[4]

It is their firm belief that

> rules wer made first by wise men, not wise men by rules.[5]

The work of Wilson and Ascham is the fruit of their association with Cheke. The results of his impact upon other minds are articulated by these men and made accessible

---

[1] Letter prefixed to his translation of Demosthenes, projected by him and Cheke in 1556.
[2] *Toxophilus* (1545), ed. W. A. Wright (1904), p. 45.   [3] *Scholemaster, op. cit.*, p. 278.
[4] Wilson, *Arte of Rhetorique*, fol. 84ᵛ.   [5] *Ibid.*, fol. 85ʳ.

to a wider public. His was the germinal personality, as they all realized and as Ascham explains in *Toxophilus:*

> And when I consider howe manye men he succoured with his helpe, & hys ayde to abyde here for learninge, and howe all men were prouoked and styrred vp, by his councell and daylye example, howe they shulde come to learning, surely I perceyue that sentence of Plato to be true, which sayeth that there is nothyng better in any common wealthe, than that there shoulde be alwayes one or other, excellent passyng man, whose lyfe and vertue, shoulde plucke forwarde the will, diligence, laboure and hope of all other, that folowyng his footesteppes, they myght comme to the same ende, wherevnto labour, lerning & vertue, had cōueied him before.[1]

Cheke's own progressive desire to restore to Greek its lost euphony brought him into conflict with the reactionary forces of authority in Cambridge. He and Sir Thomas Smith were dissatisfied with the pronunciation which made all the vowel sounds so 'closely allied to the letter *iota*'[2] that they resembled 'the piping of a sparrow, or the hissing of a snake'[3] and introduced the more classical and varied vowel sounds into their lectures and private teaching. In 1542 Stephen Gardiner, Bishop of Winchester, issued a decree forbidding the use of Cheke's amended usage,

> and thus not only stopped the new pronunciation in spite of the remonstrances of almost all the university, but almost wholly extinguished all the zeal for learning which had been kindled up among us.[4]

As Ascham seems to realize, more issues were at stake than the pronunciation of Greek alone. The opposition of Gardiner, 'yielding to the requests of certain envious men'[5] is a reminder of the forces which worked resolutely against all innovation. Men of more liberal and advanced views had always to meet an obstructive party, which did all it could to stem the tide of the new scholarship.

---

[1] *Toxophilus, op. cit.*, p. 45.
[2] Translation of letter of Roger Ascham to Brandesby (Cambridge, 1542–43). *Works*, ed. Giles (1865), Vol. 1, Part 1, Introduction, p. xxxviii.
[3] *Ibid.*, p. xxxviii. [4] *Ibid.*, p. xxxvii. [5] *Ibid.*

THE UNIVERSITIES

On the other hand, the very strenuousness of the opposition admits the menace to the old régime and habits of thought. Within a comparatively short time, Cheke's activities had made sweeping changes in the intellectual life at Cambridge. The heyday of Cambridge in the Tudor period lasted from the 'forties until about 1553.[1] The 'forties had witnessed the advances made towards the study of '*Aristotle, Plato, Tullio,* and *Demosthenes.*'[2] For the study of those four, 'the fowre pillars of learning,' Cambridge then gave place to 'no vniuersitie, neither in France, Spaine, Germanie, nor Italie.'[3] Obscurantism had therefore good cause to fear the activities of Cheke and his circle.

The influence of Cheke would have been less productive and of less importance to the development of critical consciousness in English, had it been confined to the domain of purely classical scholarship. He would still have been a stimulus to others, but less directly. As it is, his contemporaries praise his excellent mastery of the English language as highly as his skill in Greek and Latin. Wilson says that

> better skill he had in our English speach to iudge of the Phrases and properties of wordes, and to diuide sentences: than any else had that I haue knowne.[4]

Sir Thomas Smith, who shared Cheke's attempt to restore Greek pronunciation, shared also his reputation for English. He was

> also, during his residence in Cambridge, a great refiner of the English writing. which to these times was too rough and unpolished, and little care taken thereof.... He was noted to be one of the three there, that were the great masters of the English tongue.[5]

---

[1] 'S. Iohnes stoode in this state, vntill those heuie tymes, and that greuous change that chanced. An. 1553....' Ascham, *Scholemaster*, p. 280.
[2] *Ibid.*, p. 281.   [3] *Ibid.*, p. 282.
[4] Letter prefixed to translation of Demosthenes, sig. i^r.
Cf. also Nicolls' translation of Thucydides addressed to Cheke's critical judgment, 'to amende and correct it, in those places and sentences, whiche youre exacte lernynge and knolaige shall Iudge mete to be altered and refourmed.' *Op. cit.*, sig. A iii^r.
[5] Strype, *Life of Sir Thomas Smith* (1820), p. 20.

EARLY TUDOR CRITICISM

In the same way as they had tried to reform the pronunciation of Greek, they attempted also to introduce a more consistent system of spelling into the English language. Smith explains his methods in the small discourse *De Recta et Emendata Scriptione Linguae Anglicanae* (*c.* 1542).[1] Cheke wrote no similar treatise, but his spelling in his translation of the Gospel of St. Matthew and part of the first chapter of the Gospel according to St. Mark (*c.* 1550) is comparatively consistent throughout. This practical attention to the English language is a realization that it might be fitted for literary purposes if organized on a basis similar to that of the classical languages. As compared with the later complacent upholders of English these men are cautious in their examination of its defects. Their attempts to reconcile some of the anomalies of spelling had no appreciable influence, but their realization of the need for this reform is significant and valuable in their age. It is an indication that the English language was being accorded a scholarly consideration which had before been reserved for the classical languages alone. Cheke and Smith brought to their examination of English a keen sense of literary excellence and of the necessity for careful choice of language for literary purposes. Perception of the essential character of Greek prompted their attempts to reform its pronunciation and they directed a similar faculty to the study of English.

That men of such remarkable intellectual stature in their day should concern themselves with the welfare of a vernacular tongue proves the growing prestige of the English language. Brought up in the tradition of Latin as the learned language, the means of intercourse and correspondence between scholars of all nations and of access to the riches of the past, they made no light choice in taking notice of 'Englishe mater in the Englishe tongue, for Englishe men.'[2] The work of this influential nucleus of scholars is indubitably a step forward towards the final re-instatement of English as a literary language in the full Tudor period.

[1] ed. Dr. Otto Deibel (1913). See also Strype, *op. cit.*, p. 183.   [2] *Toxophilus*, p. x.

THE UNIVERSITIES

The interest of the Cambridge circle in the English language is all the more important because of the growing contemporary interest in fashions of speech. The careful critical habit of the Cambridge scholars enabled them to discriminate the elements among all these fashions which would finally be best to maintain the integrity of the English language.

The fashion for aureate language, the adornment of speech with

> ... taffeta phrases, silken terms precise,
> Three piled hyperboles, spruce affectation

had persisted strongly throughout the late fifteenth and early sixteenth centuries and its use seems to have been very widely prevalent in the mid-sixteenth century. Leland remarks that

> except truth be delycately clothed in purpure her written very-tees can scant fynde a reader.[1]

Rhetoric was still equated with ornate language rather than with the science of appropriate expression, while

> he that can catche an ynke horne terme by the taile, hym thei compt to bee a fine Englishe man, and a good Rhetorician.[2]

The tendency of this fashion is to make no reconciliation of words and matter at all. The correction of this fault seemed to lie in the establishing of a clear distinction between the language of prose and the language of poetry. Confusion of the usage of these two *genres* was a fault condemned by the rhetoricians themselves. Sherry maintains that 'if a man in prose would vse figures poeticall,'[3] he is guilty of a fault of 'ungarnished' speech, 'when eyther there lacketh order, or beautifying in the wordes.'[4] Ascham cites Cicero's calling of Sulpitius '*grandis et tragicus Orator*' for his 'Poeticall kinde of talke' as being 'for other mens warning, to eschew the like faulte,'[5] and praises Plato's use of Homer's *Iliad*

---

[1] *Antiquities* (1545).   [2] Wilson, *Arte of Rhetorique*, fol. 86ᵛ.
[3] *Op. cit.*, sig. B. iiᵛ.   [4] *Ibid.*, sig. B.iʳ.   [5] *Scholemaster*, p. 254.

Bk. I, in *De Republica* Bk. 3, because he 'doth not ride a loft in Poeticall termes, but goeth low and soft on foote, as prose and *Pedestris oratio* should do.'[1] The correct choice between the two styles should be made by the discriminating faculty working according to the demands of

> *Decorum*, which as it is the hardest point, in all learning, so is it the fairest and onelie marke, that scholers, in all their studie, must alwayes shote at. . . .[2]

Another way of surrounding meaning in a cloud of words was the use of an archaic and pedantic vocabulary. Erasmus speaking through the mouth of Folly describes the absurdity of extreme antiquarian researches:

> If they want such farre fetched vocables, than serche they out of some rotten Pamphlet foure or fyue disused woordes of antiquitee, therewith to darken the sence unto the reader, to the ende, that who so vnderstandeth theim, may repute hym selfe for more cunnyng, and literate: and who so dooeth not, shall so muche the rather yet esteeme it to be some high mattier, because it passeth his learnyng. For this is truely not the least of my pleasant propretees, to make men euer set moste store by straunge and outlandisshe thyngs.[3]

The vicissitudes of Chaucer's reputation have a place in these linguistic fashions. A vogue for the interlarding of conversation with Chaucerian expressions appears for a time in the kaleidoscope of court fashions, during which time the 'fine Courtier wil talke nothyng but Chaucer.'[4]

Another habit deplored by scholars of the judicious persuasion is that of giving a strange flavour to language by incorporating technical terms in large numbers. Law, for instance, is

> inuolued in so barbarouse a langage, that it is nat onely voyde

---

[1] *Scholemaster*, p. 255.   [2] *Ibid.*, p. 249.
[3] *Praise of Folly*, translated by Sir Thomas Chaloner (1549), p. 3.
Cf. *Quintilian*: 'At obscuritas fit verbis iam ab usu remotis: ut si commentarios quis pontificum et vetustissima foedera et exoletos scrutatus auctores id ipsum petat ex his quae inde contraxerit, quod non intelliguntur. Hinc enim aliqui famam eruditionis adfectant, ut quaedam soli scire videantur.' *Op. cit.*, Vol. 3, p. 202.
[4] Wilson, *Arte of Rhetorique*, fol. 86ᵛ.

THE UNIVERSITIES

of all eloquence, but... serueth to no commoditie or necessary purpose, no man understandyng it but they whiche haue studyed the lawes.[1]

Wilson includes the lawyer in the ranks of those whose language is extravagant as one who 'wil store his stomack with the pratyng of Pedlers.'[2] The conversion of Hall's *Chronicle*, which is 'quite marde with Indenture Englishe,' into 'proper, and commonlie vsed wordes'[3] is recommended by Ascham as an exercise for the making of an 'epitome.'

The existence of all these fashions of speech is a proof that in the mid-sixteenth century there is a general preoccupation with language, a self-consciousness which assigned great importance to the exploitation of style. Reaction against excesses added to native good sense the discipline of an informed critical outlook. Study of classical languages had awakened in scholars the sense of the essential character of each language, an exact philological sense, and these faculties, applied to English were consciously creating standards of excellence and propriety.

The use of coinages from classical languages and from contemporary vernaculars called forth another chorus of critical utterances. Excessive use of Latinized forms was considered a mark of erudition by the

> vnlearned or foolishe phantasticall, that smelles but of learnyng (suche felowes as haue seen learned men in their daies).[4]

Judged by the standards of *decorum* and lucidity, which are to the Cambridge scholars the criteria of excellence in language, these coinages are incongruous with the character of English and therefore some check must be made upon their importation. Borrowings from contemporary languages were flooding in at the same time. All Europe was 'at a great feast of languages' and each country was bent on stealing the scraps to augment its own store.

---

[1] Elyot, *Gouernour*, Vol. 1, pp. 134–135.   [2] *Arte of Rhetorique*, fol. 86r-v.
[3] *Scholemaster*, p. 260.   [4] Wilson, *Arte of Rhetorique*, fol. 86v.

EARLY TUDOR CRITICISM

This practice of speaking a cosmopolitan hotch-potch of language is quickly reflected in literature. Erasmus says:

> The Rhethoriciens of these daies ... plainely thynke theim selves demygods, if lyke horsleches thei can shew two tongues, I meane to mingle their writings with words sought out of strange langages, as if it were alouely thyng for theim to poudre theyr bokes with ynkehorne termes, although perchaunce as unaptly applied, as a gold rynge in a sowes nose.[1]

To those who advocate the incorporation of new words as well as to those who consider it injudicious, the critical touchstone is *decorum*, the sense of the preservation of linguistic integrity. Castiglione, considering the similar problem in the Italian language, makes usage his criterion. He recognizes the importance of governing the importation of new words by some definite law and decides that they will

> afterward remaine or decaye, according as they are admitted by custome or refused.[2]

Cheke enters the controversy with a statement of the position marked by his usual caution and good sense. He is strongly of the opinion that English should be preserved

> cleane and pure, unmixt and unmangeled with borowing of other tunges. . . .[3]

He is forced, however, to agree with Du Bellay's conclusion that it may

> aux nouvelles choses estre necessaire importer nouveaux mots. . . .[4]

and so advises the language to

> borow with suche bashfulnes, that it mai appeer, that if either the mould of our oun tung could serve us to fascion a woord of our oun, or if the old denisoned wordes could content and ease this neede, we wold not boldly venture of unknowen wordes.[5]

---

[1] *Praise of Folly, op. cit.*, p. 3. [2] *Op. cit.*, p. 19.
[3] *A Letter of Syr J. Cheekes To his loving frind Mayster Thomas Hoby*, prefixed to Hoby's *Courtyer, op. cit.*, p. 12.
[4] *Op. cit.*, p. 137. [5] Cheke's letter to Hoby, *op. cit.*, pp. 12-13.

THE UNIVERSITIES

Wilson welcomes the influx of new material rather more warmly, but refers the coinages, like Castiglione, to the rule of usage:

> Now whereas wordes be receiued, as well Greke as Latine, to set furthe our meanyng in thenglishe tongue, either for lacke of store, or els because we would enriche the language: it is well doen to vse them, and no man therin can be charged for any affectacion, when all other are agreed to folowe the same waie.[1]

The men of this time find technical terms and the subtleties of philosophy and the sciences difficult to express in the English language, unused to treating these subjects with the ease of Greek and Latin. The same difficulty was experienced by the Romans in transferring Greek knowledge to the Latin tongue and there is a precedent for the practice of borrowing in their solution of the problem:

> The latin men borowed of the grekes, both their knowledge and also many names of arte, bicause there is not the lyke grace of facilitie in composition, in the latyne tonge, as there is in the greeke tongue.[2]

Therefore the schoolmaster in Record's *Castle of Knowledge* says that he can give the scientific terms

> no englishe names, bicause no one woorde can aptly expres these properties, excepte I woulde triflinglye make suche an immitation.[3]

The answer of the 'Scholler' to this announcement expresses the attitude of all those who were conscious of the deficiencies of the English language:

> That imitation semeth straunge, yet were it better to make new english names, than to lacke words: therfore I will not refuse to vse them, till I can learn more apt names.[4]

That the habit of borrowing foreign words may augment the language without distorting it is acknowledged by those

---
[1] *Arte of Rhetorique*, fol. 87ᵛ.
[2] Robert Record, *Castle of Knowledge* (1556), sig. H. iiiʳ.
Cf. Quintilian, *op. cit.*, Vol. 1, pp. 104–110; Vol. 3, pp. 226–230.
[3] *Ibid.*   [4] *Ibid.*

EARLY TUDOR CRITICISM

who examined the process of adoption keenly. By some alteration borrowed words can be given a native flavour, so that they have no appearance of incongruity, for it is incontrovertible that we have

> a great nombre of other substantives and adjectives, whiche in dede be very frenche wordes, saufe that our Englyshe tong hath some thyng altred theyr later terminations, but after theyr trewe orthographie and ryght pronunciatyon be ones knowen, they be by any parson of our tong parceyved and also lerned at ones, and that for ever after.[1]

Exploration of the possibilities of the English language for the reception of new words was consciously carried out by Sir Thomas Elyot. He tries to examine the problem by practice in *The Gouernour* as a general proof of the adaptability of the language and says that

> in the redynge therof [Henry VIII] sone perceyued, that I intended to augment our Englyshe tongue, wherby men shoulde as well expresse more abundantly the thyng that they conceiued in theyr hertes (wherfore language was ordeined) hauyng wordes apte for the purpose: as also interprete out of greke, latin or any other tonge into Englysshe, as sufficiently, as out of any one of the sayde tongues into an other.[2]

As a guide to those who might perhaps be puzzled at his new formations, he adopts the honest practice of indicating them clearly, so that there is not one which is not

> there declared as playnly by one mene or other to a diligent reder that no sentēce is therby made darke or harde to be vnderstande.[3]

It has been noted that 'an analysis of forty pages of the Shorter Oxford Dictionary has shown that of every hundred words in use in 1600, thirty-nine were introduced between 1500 and 1600.'[4] This is statistical proof of the fertility of this

---

[1] *The Epistell of Andrewe Baynton*, prefixed to John Palsgrave's *L'Esclaircissement de la langue françoyse* (1530), ed. F. Génin (*Collection de Documents Inédits sur l'Histoire de France*, 1852), p. xii.
[2] *The Knowledge that Maketh a Wise Man* (1552), ' Proheme,' sig. A. iii^(r-v).
[3] *Ibid.*
[4] F. W. Bateson, *English Poetry and the English Language* (1934), p. 28.

period and justifies the efforts of those scholars who tried to increase resources of language as fully and as judiciously as possible. Elyot may claim to be one of those who made a large contribution to it.

Insistence such as that laid by Cheke on the preservation of a vocabulary mainly Saxon ignored the previous history of the language. In the Anglo-Saxon period a still flexible compound-forming habit had enabled writers such as Aelfric to forge successful native equivalents of Latin and foreign terms, and thus to keep borrowing within just limits. With the Norman Conquest and the Plantagenet rulers, however, came an incalculable influx of French words and a fusion of both languages was made with extensive increase of vocabulary for the English language. By the time when the Cambridge circle were occupied with problems of language the vernaculars in Europe were strongly asserting their claims to recognition as fit for literary production and were eager to borrow from classical languages and other sources anything which would augment their range.

At such a time a critical judgment was more than ever essential. It alone could enforce discernment in the adoption and treatment of new words when so many writers ignored this necessity and, as Ascham says,

> vsinge straunge wordes as latin, french and Italian, do make all thinges darke and harde.[1]

The consequent obscurity defeats the ends of the writers responsible for the diffusion of the lately recovered classical knowledge, which had to reach as wide an audience as possible. Scholars and rhetoricians alike emphasize the need for a pure, lucid manner of speech, as closely allied to the clarity of the spoken word as possible, for

> wrytyng is nothinge elles, but a maner of speache, that remaineth stil after a man hath spoken, or (as it were) an Image, or rather the life of the woordes.[2]

[1] *Toxophilus*, p. xiv.   [2] Hoby, *op. cit.*, p. 64.

The norm of literary composition is the fusion of organized material with simple expression, the method to achieve this being

> to speak as the cōmon people do, to thinke as wise men do: and so shoulde euery man vnderstande hym, and the iudgement of wyse men alowe hym.[1]

The distinguishing characteristic of men sensitive to these standards is the 'skilfull Iudgement' which is the faculty primarily critical. Only men with this power can create a standard literary speech:

> The good use of speache ... ariseth if men that have wytte, and with learninge and practise have gotten a good judgement, and with it consent and agree to receave the woordes that they think good, which are knowen by a certaine naturall judgement, and not by art or anye maner rule.[2]

Du Bellay in France advises choice of language by the same rules of euphony, selection and usage. In his advice to the writer he says,

> ... je renvoie tout au jugement de ton oreille. Quant au reste, use de mots purement francais, non toutefois trops communs, non point aussi trop inusites. ...[3]

The stuff of everyday intercourse is to be the basis of the literary language, for this must be its integral and characteristic framework:

> Every speach stādeth by vsual wordes, that be in vse of daily talke, and proper wordes that belong to the thing.[4]

This vocabulary will not smell of the lamp, but will be the spontaneous expression of the thought and will be reconciled with scholarly requirements by the writer's observance of the rules of *decorum*. For this reason Castiglione goes so far as to say that

[1] Ascham, *Toxophilus*, p. xiv.
Cf. Quintilian: '... Ergo consuetudinem sermonis vocabo consensum eruditorum, sicut vivendi consensum bonorum.' *Op. cit.*, Vol. 1, p. 132.
'Nobis prima sit virtus perspicuitas, propria verba, rectus ordo, non in longum dilata conclusio, nihil neque desit superfluat: ita sermo et doctis probabilis et planus imperitis erit.'
Op. cit., Vol. 3, p. 208.
[2] Hoby, *op. cit.*, p. 73.   [3] *Op. cit.*, p. 139.   [4] Sherry, *op. cit.*, sig. A. iii^v.

THE UNIVERSITIES

it is alwayes a vice to use woordes that are not in commune speach.[1]

Writers who had the welfare of the vernacular at heart were conscious of the new comparative standards with which the study of classical literature and language had supplied them. The relationship of the vernaculars to each other and to Latin was clearer to them than it had been during the period when the vernaculars were completely obscured by the domination of Latin as the universal language. They have the stimulus of linguistic achievement in other countries and the ultimate aim of excellence in the vulgar tongues similar to that of Latin and Greek. Du Bellay has high hopes of the future of the French language:

> Le temps viendra (peut estre) et je l'espere moyennant la bonne destinee francoise . . . que nostre langue . . . qui commence encore a jetter des racines, sortira de terre, et s'eslevera en telle hauteur et grosseur, qu'elle se pourra egaler aux mesmes Grecs et Romains, produisant comme eux des Homeres, Demosthenes, Virgiles et Cicerons.[2]

Before such a literature could be produced, the tempering and preparation of the language to be a fit medium was imperative. This had to be undertaken according to definite criteria, by means of which a style to meet all literary requirements could be fashioned. Deliberate formative and selective pressure had to be brought to bear upon the molten mass of vocabulary and style. In England, this control is exercised in the sixteenth century by the men of the Cambridge circle. Keeping abreast of the linguistic fashions of the time, testing, examining, making careful decisions for the best future course of the language, their aim is the creation of a standard literary speech from the results of their investigations. They are aware that

> either we must make a difference of Englishe, and saie some is learned Englishe, and other some is rude Englishe, or the one is courte talke, the other is coutrey speache, or els we must of

[1] *Op. cit.*, p. 19.   [2] *Op. cit.*, p. 66.

necessitee, banishe al suche affected Rhetorique, and vse altogether one maner of lāguage.[1]

This is the spirit and accent of the mid-Tudor world; it in no way diminishes the critical achievement of these men that in the succeeding Elizabethan phase, though the Cambridge tradition was continued by men such as Puttenham and Mulcaster, changes of fashion gave a new lease of life to 'affected Rhetorique' and deferred for many years the coming of the 'one maner of lāguage.'

[1] Wilson, *Arte of Rhetorique*, fol. 87ᵛ.

CHAPTER VI

THE RELATIONS OF RHETORIC AND LITERARY CRITICISM

THE subject of rhetoric and its modifications during the Renascence period embraces many of the problems and interests, both literary and linguistic, of the fifteenth and sixteenth centuries. Throughout the Middle Ages, knowledge of grammar and rhetoric, both bearing upon language and therefore necessarily upon the reading of classical authors, was transmitted, though fragmentarily, for the guidance of poets in the many *Artes Poetriae* and *Artes Versificatoriae*.[1] There were periods during the Middle Ages when attention to style became exaggerated to the point of preciosity and when logic and dialectic obscured the study of authors, but, whatever its vicissitudes, there was a certain continuity of attention to language. Rhetorical literature was among the classical work recovered during the Renascence and a new phase begins with the reading of Quintilian and other sources. More carefully balanced and controlled study of language ensued and brought about at the same time a more humane view of literature.[2] The mass of knowledge can only be of use if it may be broken up, logically examined and exhibited in clear, cogent and appropriate language.[3] The men of the Renascence period looked to the example of the ancient writers, whose work was now easily accessible in printed editions. The study of rhetoric was established on a broader

---

[1] For reprints of some of these treatises, see E. Faral, *Les arts poétiques du XIIième et du XIIIième siècle: recherches et documents sur la technique littéraire du moyen âge*. (Paris, 1924.)

[2] Cf. Quintilian. Of literary study, he says: '. . . nisi oratoris futuri fundamenta fideliter iecit, quidquid superstruxeris, corruet.' *Op. cit.*, Vol. 1, p. 64.

[3] Cf. Wilson, '. . . an eloquēt man beyng finally learned, can do muche more good in perswading, by shift of wordes and mete placyng of matter: then a greate learned clerke shalbe able with great store of learnyng, wantyng wordes to set furth his meanyng.' *The Arte of Rhetorique*, fol. 85ᵛ.

basis than that of mediaeval times. At its best, it comprehended the whole prose art of translating matter into words, of securing clarity of thought in language correspondingly direct.

The power of convincing and persuasive address was particularly important in an age when the scholar-prince had to play so large a part in the world of affairs. In Italy, for instance, the despots of the small city-states had to sustain their authority by force of personality and persuasion. Eloquence could not therefore moulder unused in a mere academic study of classical languages. The habit of mind moulded by this reading had to be brought to bear upon contemporary problems and a similar mastery had to be acquired over the vernacular in which the man in authority had to deal with his subordinates. The orators of Greece and Rome had explored the possibilities of all varieties of address and had carefully organized and explained their methods. Rhetoric, therefore, takes a high place in the educational system of the nobleman. In England the responsibilities of the ruling class were many and those most sensitive to new demands were eager to make the most of the opportunities of culture offered to them by the resources of printing. The Tudor age was one in which controversy of all kinds was active and the educated nobleman joined in the exchange of opinion with alacrity if his background of knowledge were sufficient. Training in the administrative duties of the ' gouernour' was naturally an essential part of his education. The qualities of the man of affairs and the man of letters were to be found in Quintilian's ideal orator.[1] They are to be gathered from wide and carefully chosen reading, for in

> an oratour is required to be a heape of all maner of lernyng: whiche of some is called the worlde of science, of other the

---

[1] 'Neque enim hoc concesserim, rationem rectae honestae vitae (ut quidam putaverunt) ad philosophos relegandam, cum vir ille vere civilis et publicarum privatarumque rerum administrationi accommodatus qui regere consiliis urbes, fundare legibus, emendare iudiciis possit, non alius sit profecto quam orator.' *Op. cit.*, Vol. I, p. 10.

RHETORIC AND LITERARY CRITICISM

circle of doctrine, which is in one worde of greke *Encyclopaedia*.[1]

The aspect of rhetoric which belongs closely to literature is its persuasive aim and the choice of style to bring about this effect. Sir Thomas Elyot considers this most important and would instruct

> the childe in that parte of rhethorike, principally, which concerneth persuation. for as moche as it is moste apte for consultations.[2]

Both rhetoric and poetic aim at compelling the intellectual and emotional assent of their audiences by combining pleasure, which holds their attention, and instruction, which convinces them of the value of the matter offered. This process is implied in the three-fold aim of rhetoric[3] agreed upon by classical writers and adopted into the Renascence period. Wilson states the purpose early in his *Arte of Rhetorique*:

> Three thynges are required of an Orator.
> - To teache.
> - To delight.
> - And to perswade.[4]

and Elyot reproduces the classical idea in his definition of rhetoric:

> Undoubtedly very eloquence is in euery tonge where any mater or acte done or to be done is expressed in wordes clere, propise, ornate and comely: whereof sentences be so aptly compact that they by a vertue inexplicable do drawe unto them the mindes and consent of the herers, they beinge therwith either perswaded, meued, or to delectation induced.[5]

The effect of persuasion depends largely upon style. After the preliminary activity of choosing the subject matter (*Inventio*), and of arranging it in the best order (*Dispositio*),

---

[1] Elyot, *Gouernour*, Vol. 1, p. 118.
Cf. Quintilian: 'Ego (neque id sine auctoribus) materiam esse rhetorices iudicio omnes res quaecumque ei ad dicendum subiectae sunt.' *Op. cit.*, Vol. 1, p. 356.
[2] *Ibid.*, Vol. 1, p. 118.
[3] Cf. Quintilian: 'Oratoris officium docendi, movendi, delectandi....' *Op. cit.*, Vol. 3, p. 180.
[4] Fol. iv. [5] Elyot, *op. cit.*, Vol. 1, pp. 116–117.

EARLY TUDOR CRITICISM

the function of *Elocutio* is to place the best words in the best order.[1] The classical precepts are faithfully transmitted and used from the earliest Tudor phase onwards.

Caxton in his translation of the French encyclopaedia *Image du Monde* transmits advice for the right ordering of *elocutio*:

> The third thing is eloque*n*s, as wha*n* thou haste disposed how euery poynt & mat*er* shalbe shewed in ordre than thou must vtt*er* it with fayr eloque*nt* wordes, and not to vse many curyous termes, for sup*er*fluyte in euery thyng is to be dyspraysed; And it hyndreth the sente*n*ce. And whan a man delatith his matt*er* to long or that he vtt*er* the effecte of his sentence, though it be neuer so well vtteryd, it shalbe tedyous vnto the herers; for euery ma*n* naturally that hereth a nother, desyreth moste to know the effecte of his reason that tellyth the tale. . . . Therfor the pryncypall poynt of eloquens reityth [restyth] euer in the quycke sentence. And therfor the lest poynt belonging to Rethorike is to take hede that the tale be quycke & sentencious.[2]

Stephen Hawes among the poets reproduces the mediaeval conception of the rhetorical system with little modification. He explains:

> And than the .iii. parte / is elocucyon
> Whan inuencyon / hath the purpose wrought
> And set it in ordre / by dysposycyon
> Without this thyrde parte / it vayleth ryght nought
> Thoughe it be founde / and in ordre brought
> Yet elocucyon / with the power of Mercury
> The mater exorneth / ryght well facundyously
>
> In fewe wordes / swete and sentencyous
> Depaynted with golde / harde in construccyon
> To the artyke eres / swete and dylycyous

---

[1] Cf. Quintilian: 'Eloqui enim est omnia, quae mente conceperis, promere atque ad audientes perferre; sine quo supervacua sunt priora et similia gladio condito atque intra vaginam suam haerenti.' *Op. cit.*, Vol. 3, p. 184.

[2] *Myrrour and dyscrypcyon of the worlde, with many meruaylles of the vii. scyences As Gramayre, Rethorike, with the arte of memorye, etc.* (1481). From reprint of *c.* 1527, quoted F. I. Carpenter, *op. cit.*, pp. 25–26.

Cf. Quintilian: '[Elocutio] spectatur verbis aut singulis aut coniunctis. In singulis intuendum est ut sint . . . perspicua, ornata, ad id quod efficere volumus accommodata. . . .' *Op. cit.*, Vol. 3, p. 194.

RHETORIC AND LITERARY CRITICISM

The golden rethoryke / is good refeccyon
And to the reder / ryght consolacyon....[1]

The conception and importance of *elocutio* varied. The poets and prose writers of the late fifteenth and early sixteenth centuries were preoccupied with matters of style. When they use the term 'rhetoric' they usually signify *elocutio*, since it provided them with the means of achieving the 'aureate' style in verse and ornamental prose. They drew upon the laws of composition preserved in mediaeval textbooks such as Geoffroi de Vinsauf's *Nova Poetria*,[2] from whom Chaucer says he derived his knowledge of rhetoric.[3] Chaucer's allusions to rhetorical practice seem to indicate that it stood even then primarily for elaboration and ornamentation of language.[4] This conception persisted in the fifteenth and early sixteenth centuries, when there was a strong feeling for the 'high style' in Europe, and in English poetry for a time no less than elsewhere.

The Scottish Chaucerians are past masters in this art. William Dunbar uses the term 'rethor' for poet, giving Chaucer praise for the elegance of his language:

> O, reverend Chaucer, ross of rethouris all,
> As in our toung ane flour imperiall,
>   That raiss in Britane evir, quha reidis richt,
> Thow beiris of makaris the tryvmph royall;
> Thy fresch ennammallit termes celestiall
>   This mater cowth have illuminit full bricht....[5]

and tributes to Gower and Lydgate are due to their 'angelic mowth[is] most mellifluat,'[6] which

---

[1] *Op. cit.*, p. 40, ll. 904–915.   [2] See E. Faral, *op. cit.*
[3] *The Nonne Preestes Tale*. (Works of Geoffrey Chaucer, ed. W. W. Skeat, 1894. *The Canterbury Tales*. Text, p. 285, ll. 4537–4541.)
For discussion of the extent of Chaucer's knowledge and use of rhetorical theory, see J. M. Manly, *Chaucer and the Rhetoricians*, Warton Lecture on English Poetry, XVII.
[4] *The Prologe of the Frankeleyns Tale* (ed. Skeat, *ibid.*, p. 481, ll. 719–726) and *the Prologe of the Clerkes Tale of Oxenforde* (ed. Skeat. *Ibid.*, p. 389, ll. 16–20).
[5] *The Goldin Terge*, Stanza 29, *The Poems of William Dunbar*, ed. H. B. Baildon (1907), p. 52, ll. 253–258.
[6] *Ibid.*, Stanza 30, l. 265.

EARLY TUDOR CRITICISM

Our rude langage hes cleir illumynat,
And fair ourgilt our speiche, that imperfyte
Stude, or 3our goldin pennis schup to wryt. . . .[1]

This adherence to the mediaeval idea is, perhaps, strengthened by the writing of elaborate addresses and epistles in the manner advocated by the *ars dictaminis* and deplored by Elyot, who says that

> euery man is nat an oratour that can write an epistle or a flatering oration in latin: where of the laste (as god helpe me) is to moche used.[2]

With a fuller understanding of the more liberal conception of rhetoric contained in the work of Cicero and Quintilian, balance was restored later in the sixteenth century as humanist study of the classics flourished. The term 'rhetoric' was then restored to its full sense, including invention and organization as well as carefully chosen speech and *elocutio* no longer demanded expression so tortuous and elaborate as to be often obscure and ungraceful.

The virtues admired by the men who respond fully to the classical tradition are succinctness, pungency, clarity. They understand the classical idea of *elocutio*, consisting in

> wordes, considered by thēselues, & when thei be ioyned together. Apt wordes by searchyng must be foūd out, and after by diligence, cōueniently coupled.[3]

It is at once the energizing and controlling factor of language. Wilson remarks,

> Many can tell their mynde in Englishe, but fewe can vse mete termes, and apt order: suche as all men should haue, and wise men will vse: suche as nedes must be had, when matters should be vttered.[4]

The man trained in rhetorical precept will cultivate this directness of speech and be able to

---

[1] *Ibid.*, ll. 266–268.   [2] *Op. cit.*, Vol. I, p. 117.
[3] Sherry, *A Treatise of the Figures of Grammar and Rhetorike*, sig. A. ii^v–A. iii^r.
Cf. Quintilian: 'Nobis prima sit virtus perspicuitas, propria verba, rectus ordo, non in longum dilata conclusio, nihil neque desit neque superfluat. . . .' *Op. cit.*, Vol. 3, p. 208.
[4] *Op. cit.*, fol. 85^v.

RHETORIC AND LITERARY CRITICISM

vtter his mind in plain wordes, suche as are vsually receiued and tell it orderly, without goyng aboute the busshe.[1]

This entails a strenuous mental discipline, to be followed out in accordance with precepts of classical writers whose example is also the standard of proficiency. To choose words

> fynely, and handsomely to bestowe them in their places, after the minde of Cicero and Quintilian, is no easye thing.[2]

These standards are valid for the usage of any language, since they depend upon the reasoned choice of men of balanced and acute minds. The diction will be that which suggests itself as springing naturally from the subject-matter, the method of selection being

> an appliyng of apte wordes and sentēces to the matter, founde out to confirme the cause.[3]

Only when 'apte woordes and vsuall Phrases to sette forthe oure meanynge'[4] have been selected can the process of ornamentation be allowed. Then, within the bounds of propriety,

> we maye boldelye commende and beautifie oure talke wyth diuers goodlye coloures, and delitefull translations, that oure speache maye seme as bryghte and precious, as a ryche stone is fayre and orient.[5]

There is, therefore, a brief period in the mid-sixteenth century when rhetoricians and men of letters admired and did their best to promulgate the use of pure, chastened diction and carefully ordered arrangement. John Jewel, Bishop of Salisbury and prelector in humanity and rhetoric at Corpus Christi College, Oxford, suffered a strong reaction against the artificiality of rhetorical method as taught in the Universities and delivered his vehement oration *Contra Rhetoricam* (*c.* 1548). This exhortation to sounder learning and purer style is in accord with the trend of the humanist

---
[1] *Op. cit.*, fol. 1ᵛ.   [2] Sherry, *op. cit.*, sig. A. iiiʳ.
[3] Wilson, *op. cit.*, fol. 4ʳ. Cf. Quintilian: 'Curam ergo verborum, rerum volo esse sollicitudinem. Nam plerumque optima rebus cohaerent et cernuntur suo lumine.' *Op. cit.*, Vol. 3, p. 188.
[4] Wilson, *op. cit.*, fol. 89ᵛ.   [5] *Ibid.*, fol. 810 [*sic*]ʳ.

EARLY TUDOR CRITICISM

rhetoricians in England. Like them he admires truth unadorned:

> Veritas enim candida et simplex est, minime opus habet linguae praesidio et eloquentia, quae si est perspicua et clara, satis habet ipsa in se firmamenti, expolitae orationis delicias non requirit: sive obscura et adversa est, non ea in clamore et cursu verborum exquiritur.[1]

This trend towards integrity and chastity of literary language was not altogether destined to be realized. In their intoxication with linguistic power and ingenuity, men of the full Elizabethan period became preoccupied with figures, schemes and tropes. It was, however, of service that the recovery of true rhetorical standards in the earlier phase of the century came at a time when systematic guidance was very necessary. The transmission of classical standards by Cox, Sherry and Wilson gave valuable stimulus and encouragement to the awakening interest in England. The men of the Cambridge Circle in which Wilson moved were attempting to evolve a standard literary language which should be acceptable to scholars and comprehensible to the unlearned. The establishment of this linguistic ideal must enhance colloquial speech, selecting, testing, rejecting, choosing the most appropriate elements. Classical precepts were available for comparison and incentive. The humanist aim was essentially that of Quintilian[2] and the English at which they aimed was to have the virtues chosen for Quintilian's standard Latin. Sir John Cheke and his supporters could find a rhetorical precedent for their views, since Quintilian had inveighed against the same danger to pure vocabulary.[3]

It is interesting to note that Cheke reacts against the contemporary devotion to Cicero and substitutes Demosthenes,

[1] *Works*, ed. R. W. Jelf, 1848, Vol. 8, p. 212.
[2] '... Sermo et doctis probabilis et planus imperitis erit.' *Op. cit.*, Vol. 3, p. 208. and: 'Consuetudo vero certissima loquendi magistra, utendumque plane sermone et nummo, cui publica forma est.' *Ibid.*, Vol. 1, p. 112.
[3] 'Peregrina porro ex omnibus prope dixerim gentibus ut homines, ut instituta etiam multa venerunt.' *Ibid.*, Vol. 1, p. 104.

RHETORIC AND LITERARY CRITICISM

because of his less mannered style. Demosthenes was well-known in Italy as early as the time of Chrysoloras, who came to Italy from Constantinople.[1] Until the appearance of the *editio princeps* from the Aldine press in 1504, he was neglected in Northern Europe where Greek studies were more intermittent. The interest of the Cambridge Circle in the study of Demosthenes is another proof of their discrimination and strong conviction in stylistic matters, particularly as regards the formation of a literary language based upon the idiom of ordinary speech. Wilson, the first English translator of Demosthenes, says in his account of Cheke's interest:

> He was moued greatly to like Demosthenes aboue all others, for that he sawe him so familiarly applying himselfe to the sense and vnderstanding of the common people, that he sticked not to say, that none euer was more fitte to make an English man tell his tale praise worthily in any open hearing, either in Parlament or in Pulpit, or otherwise, than this onely Orator was.[2]

To the stimulus of Sir John Cheke, English scholarship owes also the knowledge of Aristotle's *Rhetorica* and *Poetica*. The *Rhetorica* was apparently unused in Western Europe from Roman times until the fourteenth century.[3] During the fifteenth century, new Greek manuscripts were brought to Europe by scholars and travellers and in 1508-9 Aldus issued the *editio princeps* of both these works, while in 1531 Erasmus helped with the Basel edition, the first complete Greek edition to include the two.[4] The influence of Aristotle does not, however, seem to have progressed very quickly. The two early English rhetoricians, Leonard Cox and Richard Sherry, rely in the main upon their respective models, Melancthon's *Institutiones Rhetoricae* (1521) and Erasmus' *De duplici copia verborum* (1529) and draw freely

[1] See *Demosthenes and his Influence*, C. D. Adams, 1927, p. 131.
[2] *Op. cit.*, sig. j.ʳ⁻ᵛ.
[3] See M. T. Herrick, 'The History of Aristotle's Rhetoric in England,' *Philological Quarterly*, Vol. 5, 1926, p. 243.
[4] *Ibid.*, p. 247.

upon the common Renascence stock of rhetorical knowledge in Cicero and Quintilian. Wilson's *Arte of Rhetorique* (1553) has features which may be derived from Aristotle—the division into three books, the three-fold consideration of rhetoric as demonstrative, deliberative and judicial—but, since these are also found in Cicero and Quintilian, they are not in themselves conclusive proof that Wilson was using Aristotle.[1] The assumption that he was is supported by the similarity of some passages in each[2] and the fact that Cheke is known to have used both the *Rhetorica* and the *Poetica*.[3] The English rhetoricians draw upon a background wide and sound for their day.

Rhetoric is important in the development of the critical spirit in the Early Tudor period because it provides expression and definition for the literary and linguistic interests of the age. Leonard Cox, whose *Arte or Craft of Rhethoryke* was probably written about 1530,[4] belongs to a period rather too early for the interest in style which is the main concern of Sherry, Wilson and the Cambridge Circle. He supplies, however, the full discipline of *inventio* and *dispositio*, emphasizing the need for clear arrangement before the graces of style could follow.[5] As a schoolmaster[6] he realizes the need for the use of the vernacular in instruction and hopes that his work will

> do some pleasure and ease to suche as haue by neclygence or els false parsuasyons be put to the lernynge of other scyences or euer [A iii b] they haue attayned any meane knowledge of the latyne tonge.[7]

The work of Sherry and Wilson passes to the more detailed consideration of style and under their auspices the study of

---

[1] See M. T. Herrick, *op. cit.*, pp. 248–249.   [2] *Ibid.*
[3] See Ascham, Letter to Brandesby, Cambridge, 1542–1543. *Op. cit.*, Vol. 1, p. 26, and *Scholemaster*, pp. 284, 289.
[4] For the reasons for assigning it to this date see F. I. Carpenter, *op. cit.*, pp. 9, 12.
[5] Cf. Cicero: '... nisi *res* est ab oratore percepta et cognita, inanem quandam habet elocutionem et paene puerilem.' *De Oratore*, I.6, ed A. S. Wilkins (1892), Vol. 1, p. 88, l. 15–p. 89, l. 2.
[6] He was appointed master of the grammar school of Reading, Berks, in 1530. *Op. cit.*, p. 12.
[7] *Ibid.*, p. 42.

RHETORIC AND LITERARY CRITICISM

rhetoric is laid down on lines which aim at the promotion of a good, workmanlike English style, transferring what had originally been the requirements of the Roman and Greek orators to the literary language. The men of the sixteenth century were quick to see the connection between the written and the spoken word. Du Bellay, attempting to codify rules for the improvement of the French language, says that

> le poète et l'orateur sont comme les deux piliers qui soutienne l'edifice de chacune langue[1]

and therefore addresses his work to them both:

> Tout ce que j'ay dit pour la defense et illustration de nostre langue appartient principalement à ceux qui font profession de bien dire, comme les poëtes et les orateurs.[2]

Rhetoric is the means of cultivating sure taste and sharpening mental abilities, for the conviction was growing that 'le style, c'est l'homme.' With a liberal training in rhetoric a man

> will not bee bounde to any precise rules, nor kepe any one order, but suche onely as by reason he shall thynke best to vse, beeyng maister ouer Arte, rather then Arte shoulde be maister ouer hym. . . . For what mattereth whether we followe our Booke, or no, if wee folowe witte, and appoint our selfe an order, suche as may declare the truthe more plainly?[3]

Ascham describes the resulting habit of mind as the ability to

> worke a true choice and placing of wordes, a right ordering of sentences, an easie vnderstandyng of the tonge, a readines to speake, a facultie to write, a true iudgement, both of his owne, and other mens doinges, what tonge so euer he doth use.[4]

Perhaps there was in Ascham's mind some thought of the attainments of Sir John Cheke. Also he may well be among those of Wilson's acquaintance who

> haue suche a gift in the Englishe, as fewe in Latine haue the like and therfore, delite the wise and lerned so muche, with

[1] *Op. cit.*, p. 111.   [2] *Ibid.*, p. 91.   [3] Wilson, *op. cit.*, fol. 84ᵛ.   [4] *Scholemaster*, p. 183.

EARLY TUDOR CRITICISM

their pleasaunt composicion: that many reioyce, when thei maie heare suche, and thynke muche learnyng is gotte, when thei maie talke with suche,[1]

of whom there was an increasing number.

As well as supplying the standards for literary speech, rhetoric has much in common with general rules of literary composition. It includes discussion of kinds of style and *genres* of literature.

The guiding principle of rhetoric is *decorum*, the law which enjoins the choice of appropriate words and the maintenance of selected style for each subject.[2] It is from this principle that there spring the divisions of the literary kinds, first distinguished by their styles. Bounds are carefully preserved between the language of prose and that of poetry, as a main distinction.[3] This principle becomes particularly important in the Renascence period when the tendency towards aureate language was all-pervasive. To poets a certain heightening of style is allowed,[4] but their speech must not be mingled with the language of prose.

Wilson inveighs against the affectation of pseudo-poetical speech in the prose of everyday life, as used by the 'Poeticall Clerkes,'[5] who will

> speake nothyng but quaint prouerbes, and blynd allegories, delityng muche in their owne darkenesse, especially, when none can tell what thei dooe saie.[6]

Besides this main separation of prose from poetry, there are other classifications of style which give rise to the idea of literary *genres*. Derived from the treatise *Ad Herennium* and adopted by subsequent classical rhetoricians is the

---

[1] *Op. cit.*, fol. 88ᵛ.
[2] Cf. Quintilian: '... cum sit ornatus orationis varius et multiplex conveniatque alius alii, nisi fuerit accommodatus rebus atque personis, non modo non illustrabit eam, sed etiam destruet et vim rerum in contrarium vertet.' *Op. cit.*, Vol. 4, p. 154.
[3] Cf. Aristotle, *Rhetorica*, Book 3, 1. 1404a. 9. *The Rhetoric of Aristotle* with a Commentary by E. M. Cope, edited by J. E. Sandys (1877), Vol. 3, pp. 10–11.
[4] *Ibid.*, sig. A. iiiiʳ. Cf. Du Bellay.   [5] *Op. cit.*, fol. 86v.   [6] *Ibid.*

RHETORIC AND LITERARY CRITICISM

division into the three styles, the plain, the middle and the grand style.[1] Thomas Wilson gives the typical description. He says that they are

> ... the great or mighty kind, whē we vse great wordes, or vehemēt figures:
> The smal kinde, when we moderate our heate by meaner wordes....
> The lowe kinde, when we vse no Metaphores, nor translated wordes, nor yet vse any amplificatiōs, but go plainelye to worke, and speake altogether in commune wordes.[2]

The convention varied little throughout the Middle Ages. The rhetoricians had conceived of a style appropriate for the kind of speaker[3] and this method of assigning characteristic speech, adopted and extended by Horace for the use of poets,[4] hardened gradually into an inviolable rule of *decorum* of speech.

This conception is transmitted through the Middle Ages in the various *artes poetriae*. Geoffroi de Vinsauf, for instance, explicitly connects style and social status:

> Et tales recipiunt appellationes ratione personarum vel rerum de quibus fit tractatus.[5]

John of Garland says:

> Item sunt tres styli secundum tres status hominum: pastorali vitae convenit stylus humilis, agricolis mediocris, gravis gravibus personis quae praesunt pastoribus et agricolis.[6]

---

[1] 'Sunt igitur tria genera, quae nos figuras appellamus, in quibus omnis oratio non uitiosa consumitur: unum grauem, alteram mediocrem, tertiam extenuatam uocamus. Grauis est, quae constat ex uerborum grauium magna [et] ornata constructione. Mediocris est, quae constat ex humiliore, neque tamen ex infima, et peruulgatissima uerborum dignitate. Attenuata est, quae demissa est usque ad usitatissimum puri sermonis consuetudinem.'
Rhetoricorum ad C. Herennivum libri IIII. incerto auctore. Cum correctionibus Pauli Manutii. Venetiis M D LXIIII. Liber IV. Fol. 49ʳ, l. 29–ᵛ. l. 9.
[2] *Op. cit.*, fol. 310ᵛ.
[3] Cf. Quintilian: 'Ipsum etiam eloquentiae genus alios aliud decet,' etc, *op. cit.*, p. 172.
[4]   aetatis cuiusque notandi sunt tibi mores,
        mobilibusque decor naturis dandus et annis.
Ars Poetica, ed. E. H. Blakeney, 1928, p. 28, ll. 156–157.
[5] Quoted E. Faral, *op. cit.*, p. 97.   [6] *Ibid.*

119

EARLY TUDOR CRITICISM

Gavin Douglas makes the same acknowledgement that

> The sayar eik suld weil consider this,
> His mater, and quhamto it entitillit is,
> Eftyr myne authouris wordis, we aucht tak tent
> That baith accord, and bene convenient,
> The man, the sentens, and the knychtlik stile.[1]

Ascham accepts the differentiation of *genres* by style:

> The trew difference of Authors is best knowne, *per diuersa genera dicendi*, that euerie one vsed. And therfore here I will deuide *genus dicendi*, not into these three, *Tenue, mediocre*, & *grande*, but as the matter of euerie Author requireth, as
>
> in Genus { Poeticum. Historicum. Philosophicum. Oratoricum.
>
> These differre one from an other, in choice of wordes, in framyng of Sentences, in handling of Argumentes, and vse of right forme, figure, and number, proper and fitte for euerie matter, and euerie one of these is diuerse also in it selfe, as the first.
>
> Poeticum, in { Comicum. Tragicum. Epicum. Melicum.[2]

Here the *genre* emerges quite clearly.

The Cambridge circle thus accept a comprehensive planning of the field of literary activity on the basis of rules from ancient rhetoric and poetic. This they apply to the judgment of contemporary work and Ascham's discussion of the merits of the Latin tragedy produced in England[3] on the classical model is typical of the penetrating and stimulating spirit of the exchange of ideas in University côteries. It shows that with the help of the body of classical

---
[1] *Op. cit.*, Vol. 3, p. 206, ll. 5–9.
[2] *Scholemaster*, pp. 283–284.
Cf. Quintilian: of the *genres* of literature he says: 'Sua cuique proposita lex, sua cuique decor est. Nam nec comoedia in cothurnos adsurgit, nec contra tragoedis socco ingreditur....' *op. cit.*, Vol. 4, p. 86.
[3] *Op. cit.*, p. 284.

RHETORIC AND LITERARY CRITICISM

theory a working system of literary criticism was gradually evolving in the Early Tudor period.

The classical writers who supply the Renascence period with its rules for composition call forth at the same time a consideration of the nature of the poet, of his creative impulse and of his place in the world. Elyot is advanced in his age in according to the poet divine afflatus. Throughout the mediaeval period, Poetry was required to serve the purposes of Theology by means of allegory. The conception of the poet as a 'maker' was therefore obscured. Study of the 'pagan authors,' reading of which had been allowed by the mediaeval Church only because it was the means of perfecting knowledge of the language of the Scriptures, helped in the Renascence period to add canons of aesthetic criticism to the useful, moral and theological aspects. Rhetoric and poetic in particular supplied these canons, because they elucidated the principles behind the classics themselves. Horace's *Ars Poetica* became the textbook of Renascence critics since it showed them the way to appreciate form and method for their own sake. Italy was foremost in this new method of criticism. The work of Dolce[1], Daniello[2] and Vida[3] in Italy interprets the Renascence point of view.

The Middle Ages had been constrained to emphasise an underlying truth in the guise of poetry. The poet was justified by the power to

>... conclude full closely
>Theyr fruytfull problemes / for reformacyon
>To make vs lerne / to lyue dyrectly
>Theyr good entent / and trew construccyon
>Shewynge to vs / the hole affeccyon
>Of the way of vertue / welthe and stableness.[4]

---
[1] Italian version of Horace's *Ars Poetica*, 1535.   [2] *Poetica*, 1536.
[3] *Ars Poetica*, ed. A. S. Cook in *The Art of Poetry: the poetical treatises of Horace, Vida and Boileau* (1892).
See J. E. Spingarn, *A History of Literary Criticism in the Renaissance*, 2nd edition, 1908, pp. 3–59 for discussion of literary criticism in Italy, and W. L. Bullock, 'Italian Sixteenth-Century Criticism.' *Modern Language Notes* (1926), pp. 254–263, for list of Italian critical treatises.
[4] Stephen Hawes, *op. cit.*, p. 47, ll. 1114–1119.

EARLY TUDOR CRITICISM

By men of the Renascence period the poet is allowed once more the inspiration which had made him in the classical period the *vates*. Elyot refers to Cicero's authority:

> And therefore Tulli in his Tusculane questyons supposeth that a poete can nat abundantly expresse verses sufficient and complete, or that his eloquence may flowe without labour wordes wel sounyng and plentuouse, without celestiall instinction, which is also by Plato ratified.[1]

They were too much concerned with the poet's civilizing power to be satisfied with those Horatian *dicta* where the *utile* is forgotten.[2] They valued in poetry 'high seriousness' and the range of knowledge and power behind it:

> Verily there may no man be an excellent poet nor oratour unlasse he haue parte of all other doctrine, specially of noble philosophie. And to say the trouth, no man can apprehende the very delectation that is in the leesson of noble poetes unlasse he haue radde very moche and in diuers autours of diuers lernynges.[3]

Reading of the poets perfects the culture and balance of the mature mind and at this stage of development Elyot would have

> none aunicent poete . . . excluded from the leesson of suche one as desireth to come to the perfection of wysedome.[4]

The poetry which lacks this serious purpose can contribute no benefit to mind or character and

> they that make verses, expressynge therby none other lernynge but the craft of versifyeng, be nat of aunicent writers named poetes, but onely called versifyers.[5]

The moving power of poetry is expressed through the rhetorical ideal and without it the teaching aim cannot be

---
[1] *Gouernour*, Vol. 1, p. 122.
[2]   non satis est pulchra esse poemata; dulcia sunto,
            et quocumque volent animum auditoris agunto.
Ars Poetica, op. cit., p. 25, ll. 99–100.
[3] Elyot, *Gouernour*, Vol. 1, p. 131. Cf. Cicero: 'Ac mea quidem sententia nemo poterit esse omni laude cumulatus orator, nisi erit omnium rerum magnarum atque artium scientiam consecutus.' *Op. cit.*, p. 88, ll. 12–14.
[4] *Ibid.*   [5] *Ibid.*, p. 120.

RHETORIC AND LITERARY CRITICISM

fulfilled. Since pleasure can draw and hold attention, poetry's power to delight is closely bound up with edifying effects, for

> excepte menne finde delight, thei will not long abide: delight theim, and wynne theim; werie theim, and you lose theim for euer.[1]

Quintilian had gone farther than Horace in declaring pleasure-giving to be the poet's sole aim,[2] but there had always been latent in classical tradition the acceptance of the poets as souces of various knowledge as well as of moral suasion. The Renascence stresses this and makes the instructive and cultural value of poetry one of its most important tenets.

England was much slower than Italy to absorb and formulate variations and developments in aesthetic theory. The work of the English rhetoricians, Cox, Sherry and Wilson is limited to training in the best utterance and careful structure. Cox is concerned with the setting out of the subject and the relation between Logic and Rhetoric which bears upon the clarifying of thought before Rhetoric adds the final polish:

> ... the Rhetoricyan seketh abought and boroweth when he can asmuche as he may for to make the symple and playne Logycall argumentes gay and delectable to the aere. so then the sure Judgement of argumentes or reasons muste be lernyd of the Logicyan but the crafte to set them out with plesaunte fygures and to delate the matter longith to the Rhetorycian....[3]

Sherry lays down general rules of style in 'A brief note of Eloquution the thirde parte of Rhetorike'[4] and treats the faults which impair integrity of style. Having laid the foundations, he proceeds to the complex process of selecting

> very garnyshed wordes; proper, translated, and graue sētences, which are handled in amplificatiō, comiseratio,[5]

---

[1] Wilson, *op. cit.*, fol. 2ᵛ.
[2] '... solam petit voluptatem eamque etiam fingendo non falso modo sed etiam quaedam incredibilia sectatur.' *Op. cit.*, Vol. 4, p. 18.
[3] *Op. cit.*, p. 48.   [4] *Op. cit.*, fol. iiᵛ.–fol. iiiᵛ.   [5] *Ibid.*, fol. lixᵛ.

and elaborates the kinds of figures, schemes and tropes. Wilson's *Arte of Rhetorique* is the most comprehensive of the three and bears the clear impress of the thought of the Cambridge Circle. His comments in the third book upon the contemporary linguistic fashions and affectations show that rhetorical study was not limited to the classical languages, but was seen to have some connection with vernacular problems. He refers to the contemporary activity of translation, noticing the

> large commentaries written, and the Paraphrasis of Erasmus englished.[1]

'The English Prouerbes gatherede by Jhon Heywood' serve him as an example of 'Allegory'[2] and he praises 'Sir Thomas More for his Eutopia.'[3]

There is, therefore, abundant evidence to show how the rhetoricians helped to articulate literary opinion and to provide in the terms of rhetoric inherited from the classical treatises an apparatus with which to do this. A study of the modifications of meaning and usage undergone by rhetorical terms in the course of their adoption into acknowledged literary criticism would be a valuable chart of linguistic and literary opinion. It was as well for the language of the Early Tudor period that the rhetoricians of that day were not intoxicated by their new grasp of the subject into cultivating 'the limbs and outward flourishes' of thought in elaborate language, but aimed instead at solving tangled questions with balanced and judicious care.

[1] *Op. cit.*, fol. 93^v. [2] *Op. cit.*, fol. 94^r. [3] *Ibid.*, fol. 106^r.

CHAPTER VII

EARLY TUDOR DRAMA

THERE is always in drama a certain independent element, the springs of which lie outside literature, especially the literature of critics. The impulse to dramatize emotion by miming and the dance is deep-rooted in human nature, together with the vicarious pleasure which comes from watching these spectacles. Religious ceremonial is another manifestation of formalized emotion which may develop into a *genre* of drama. These stimuli owe little to any inherited literary tradition, being recurrent, spontaneous and self-contained.

The drama of the Middle Ages in Europe derived little from Greece or Rome. Greek drama was almost entirely obscured by the fall of the Roman Empire. Latin drama survived a little more persistently in the ten tragedies of Seneca, preserved but seldom studied before the fourteenth century, and in the comedies of Terence. The works of both these dramatists were valued for their *sententiae*, easily gathered for anthologies of moral precepts and for school textbooks. The forms of Terence stimulated the imitations of Hrotsvitha, the nun of Gandersheim (tenth century),[1] but her achievement is isolated and there seems to have been no purely literary study of drama.

The second contribution of the Roman Empire was the debased form of entertainment provided by the 'mimi' and 'pantomimi,' consisting of farce and tavern by-play. From this line there is no purely literary influence. It maintained the tradition of drama as entertainment but has little importance in the study of serious literary origins.

From religious impulses there arise two branches of

---

[1] See English translations by:
H. J. W. Tillyard, *The Plays of Roswitha* (1923).
Christopher St. John, *The Plays of Roswitha* (1923).

EARLY TUDOR CRITICISM

drama in the Middle Ages. The pagan fertility rituals, of which the origins are remote in very early times, survived in various forms of folk play and symbolic dance[1] and of these a few, such as the mummers' play of St. George, become articulate drama with spoken words. From the tenth century onwards, Christianity in Western Europe develops within itself a new dramatic form from the liturgical play. This becomes the fully-grown species of vernacular drama, the miracle play presenting the pageant of the Old and New Testaments. When this development has taken place, the form may be considered separately from its religious origin. It may contain embryonic forms which, when criticism becomes self-conscious on classical lines, may be identified with the comic or the tragic. The same holds true for the morality play, but since, through its employment of Allegory it is linked to a mediaeval dominant form, since it becomes in a special degree the mouthpiece of the early Tudor period, and since, its essence being debate, it provides opportunity for the play of ideas, religious, moral, educational and social, it has to be considered primarily as the product and expression of its own age. Neo-classicism to come can too easily be allowed to cast long shadows before on a form which was alive to influences other than those of a literary movement. An attempt should be made to assess its value with a minimum of stress on ancient precedents and later critical doctrines.

The writers of the Early Tudor moralities and interludes betray no consistent literary recognition of any change of standard or standpoint. They were not making any attempt in their work to measure the potentialities of the native drama in England or to draw any comparison between it and classical drama. In contemporary France, the Pléiade and writers associated with this literary *côterie* were trying to utilize mediaeval forms and to reconsider their value in the

[1] See E. K. Chambers, *The English Folk Play* (1933).
The Mediaeval Stage (1903).
A. W. Ward, *English Dramatic Literature* (1899), Vol. I, Ch. I.

light of the newly recovered classical knowledge. Drama had its place in this process of revaluation. Thomas Sébillet, for instance, realized that there was latent in the morality a germ of the same stuff which composed tragedy. He says in 1548:

> La Moralité Françoise represente en quelque chose la Tragedie Gréque et Latine, singulierement en ce qu'elle traite fais graves et Principaus. Et si le François s'estoit rengé a ce que la fin de la Moralité fut toujours triste et douloureuse, la Moralité seroit Tragédie.[1]

Du Bellay himself was not in favour of such a compromise. He desired the creation of a French drama on the classical pattern, to replace, not to re-model, the farce and the morality:

> Quant aux comedies et tragedies, si les roys et les républiques les vouloient restituer en leur ancienne dignité, qu'ont usurpée les farces et moralities, je seroy bien d'opinion que tu t'y employasses, et si tu le veux faire pour l'ornement de ta langue, tu sçais ou tu en dois trouver les archetypes.[2]

In practice, this endeavour to destroy the indigenous morality proved ineffectual, since the native drama was strong enough to exercise an influence upon the classical forms.

The production of morality plays in England was prolific, but for a long time the form shows no apparent signs of influence from a classical source and is accorded no literary status by academic circles. It is a mingled and amorphous form, capable of ready adjustment to contemporary needs, and, through its give and take of opinions, it quickly reflects new habits of thought and new topical interests. The persistent repetition of the type shows that it satisfied a contemporary need. It is welcomed by the audience for its entertainment and by its writers for its opportunities for discussion and polemic, religious and, later, political. This

---

[1] Quoted Raymond Labègue, *La Tragédie religieuse en France: Les Débuts* (1514–1573), 1929, pp. 169 ff.
[2] *Op. cit.*, p. 109.

branch of native drama, therefore, is handling independently, or, as in the satiric debate, with French precedent, elements which may feed the critical spirit or supplement evidence of critical developments in other fields, but which are no part of any programme of conscious critical doctrine or imitation.

The serious debate is a homily in the dramatic form and can be called the moral interlude. Its main theme is the conflict between man and his circumstances in his passage through the world. This is essentially the stuff of tragedy in the Aristotelian sense of 'men in action,' but in the morality it is embodied in abstract terms. Mankind, or Everyman, whatever name is given to the representative of human life, is a vague figure. The tragic issue is never narrowed to a Hamlet or a Lear. The moral interlude is merely an extension of the sermon theme, until, at the beginning of the sixteenth century, there are indications of new life stirring in it. There are signs of a withdrawal from the rather lifeless abstractions to more particular types. For instance, among the roystering company of Freewill, Imagination and their associates in the interlude of *Hickscorner* (c. 1513) there is no figure without some distinguishing individual characteristic which removes it from the purely general.

There is a further step in the direction towards a tragic protagonist in Skelton's *Magnyfycence* (c. 1516). The main character is the representative of the limited class of those who

haue welth at wyll, largesse and lyberte.[1]

Pride in his wealth and the envisaging of the power it may bring him are the same tragic faults of *hubris* as destroy Marlowe's Barabbas. Magnyfycence boasts in almost the same terms as Marlowe's Jew. He says:

> Fortune to her lawys can not abandune me,
> But I shall of Fortune rule the reyne;
> I fere nothynge Fortunes perplexyte;
> All honour to me must nedys stowpe and lene.[2]

[1] *Poetical Works*, Vol. 1, p. 273, l. 1476. [2] *Magnyfycence, op. cit.*, p. 273, ll. 1477-1480.

EARLY TUDOR DRAMA

while Barabbas asks,

> What more may Heaven doe for earthly man
> Than thus to poure out plenty in their laps[1]

and Tamburlaine boasts:

> I hold the Fates bound fast in yron chaines,
> And with my hand turne Fortunes wheel about.[2]

When neo-classical study restored the ideal of the tragic hero, there was a tendency towards individuality which could readily adopt it. Whether in the purely native morality or in the product of a fuller Latin culture still pre-Renascence (such as Skelton's interlude), there is a general stir of interest, a progress of ideas, which go far to create the conditions in which criticism may be active.

A great deal that was purely entertaining was incorporated in the framework of the serious interlude, even tending frequently to usurp the main interest. The importance of the wooers of Lucrece in Henry Medwall's *Fulgens and Lucrece* (printed 1513-19, possibly acted 1497)[3] is quite eclipsed by the byplay of the wooers of her handmaid. The theme of Man's temptations is interspersed in Medwall's *Nature*[4] with a comic underplot. The instances of the increasing importance of the comic and the real might be multiplied throughout these early plays. The tendency to farce in native drama is reinforced by foreign example in the work of John Heywood.

Heywood is outstanding among Early Tudor dramatists for introducing interludes modelled on the French *sottie* and *débat* into the Tudor literature of entertainment.[5] Among them, *Wylly and Wyttles* (belonging to the reign of Henry VIII) is a skilful exercise in dialectic and *The Play of*

---

[1] *Works*, ed. C. F. Tucker Brooke (1910), *The Jew of Malta*, Act I, ll. 145-146, p. 245.
[2] *Ibid.*, *Tamburlaine*, Act I, sc. 2, ll. 369-370, p. 18.
[3] Henry E. Huntington Facsimile Reprints (1920).
[4] *Nature*. // *A goodly interlude of Nature copyld by mayster* // *Henry Medwall chapleyn to the ryght re-* // *uerent father in god Johan Morton* // *somtyme Cardynall and arche-* // *byshop of Can-* // *terbury* (between 1530 and 1534).
[5] See Karl Young, 'The Influence of the French farce upon the Plays of John Heywood,' *Modern Philology*, Vol. 2, (1904), pp. 97-124.

EARLY TUDOR CRITICISM

Loue (printed 1533) is an even more intricate discussion in the same 'debate' form. The *Play of the Wether* (printed 1533) has the same structure, but in the person of Meryreport there is a spirit purely humorous and the whole tone of the interlude is jocular. *The Pardoner and the Frere* (printed 1533) and *The Play called the Foure P.P.* (1552-59) are respectively a discussion of the abuses of the Church and an exercise in ingenuity treated in the same high-spirited manner. The 'shrew comedy,' *Johan Johan*, a 'mery play betwene Johan Johan the husbande Tyb his wife and Syr Jhan the preest' is the quintessence of Heywood's humour, full of Rabelaisian gusto and horse-play. Heywood writes out of the ebullience of his own nature, without regard to critical theories or tradition. His plays are 'more matter for a May morning,' using the framework of the serious interlude for purposes with no hint of the didactic or edifying in them. The stamp of individuality on his work is a novelty in the Early Tudor period, when so many plays were produced in the conventional manner.

He exults in his own capacity to amuse and delight with no *arrière pensée* :

> Art thou Heywood with the mad mery wit
> Ye forsooth maister that same is euen hit
> Art thou Heywood that applieth mirth more than thrift
> Ye sir I take mery mirth a golden gift
> Art thou Heywood that hath made many plaies
> Ye many plaies fewe good woorkes in all my daies
> Art thou Heywood that hath made men mery long
> Ye and will if I be made mery among
> Art thou Heywood that woulde be made mery now
> Ye sir helpe me to it now I beseche you.[1]

The Tudor audience was ready to listen to all kinds of discussion in the form of an interlude, finding it

> pastime convenient
> For all maner men, and a thing congruent.[2]

[1] Proverb, quoted R. de la Bère, *John Heywood, Entertainer* (1937), p. 97.
[2] *Jack Juggler*, ed. W. H. Williams (1914), Prologue, p. 3, ll. 47-48.

EARLY TUDOR DRAMA

Political interest was strong and it was soon realized that the abstract figure of mankind could be replaced by that of the state, as in *Respublica* (*c.* 1553). The aim of the play is

> To shewe that all commenweals Ruin *and* decaye
> from tyme to tyme hath been, ys, and shalbe alwaie,
> when Insolence, Flaterie, Opression,
> and Avarice have the Rewle in their possession.[1]

Miracle plays are turned to this new purpose also, as in John Bale's *Brefe comedy or enterlude of Johan Baptystes preachynge in the Wyldernesse* (1538), *The Temptacyon of our Lorde* (1538) and *God's Promises* (1538). The eagerness to adapt the dramatic form for contemporary purposes proves the existence of a lively interest in stage debate and shows how it was expected to reach men's business and bosoms. The result is that under the pressure of these new influences new dramatic forms grew up, not from an impulse directly literary, but capable of receiving literary confirmation later in their development.

When the drama turns its attention to affairs of state, the chronicle history, so important a form in the full Tudor period, comes into being. There is even a hint of the later union of history and tragedy as early as Bale's *Kyng Johan*, written in its early form in the late 1530's. From the train of events there emerges a certain sense of *nemesis*, which anticipates the inescapable coming of the wheel full circle in high tragedy.

This widening of the scope of drama to admit such a large range of subject matter, even within the mediaeval forms, gives it an unquestioned status in the Tudor world. The flexible debate form is useful for discussion of contemporary problems. A vernacular form itself, it is used for discussion concerning the use of the vernacular for other purposes. The audience to whom it is addressed was that

[1] *A merye enterlude entitled Respublica, made in the yeare of oure Lord* 1553, *and the first yeare of the moost prosperous Reigne of our moste gracious Soveraigne, Quene Marye the first.* Ed. L. A. Magnus, E.E.T.S. (Extra Series 94), 1905, Prologue, p. 1, l. 17–p. 2, l. 22.

EARLY TUDOR CRITICISM

for whose instruction men of letters of this period felt themselves responsible. John Bale in *The Thre Laws* (1538) discusses the use of the Scriptures in the vernacular. In the words of 'Avaritia' he marshals the arguments of the obscurantists who wished to withhold the interpretation of the Scriptures as the prerogative of the Church alone. Such men insist that

> ... the laye people, praye neuer but in latyne,
> Lete them haue theyr Crede, and seruyce all in latyne
> That, a latyne beleue, maye make a latyne sowle,
> Lete them nothynge knowe, of Christ, nor yet of powle
> If they have Englysh, lete it be for aduaūtage,
> For pardons, for Dyrges, for offerynges and pylgrimage.[1]

The drama is included in the far-reaching translating activity and incidental comment adds another grain to the heap of *dicta* concerning the status and possibilities of the language. The *Andria* of Terence is one of the first works of imagination to be translated in the Early Tudor period and this translation is all the more interesting and significant because it is thought to have been undertaken by John Rastell, a man whose family had at heart serious purposes concerning English drama. In the Prologue to his translation Rastell examines the progress of the English language up to his time and the linguistic problems which had arisen. He concludes that achievement in English had so far been unremarkable, either in translation or in the writing of 'bokys for ... delyte.'[2] He pays the conventional tribute to Gower, who ... of moralite ... wrote ryght craftely.[3] Chaucer he praises for his language, saying that he wrote

> as compendious & elegantly
> As in any other tong euer dyd any[4]

and echoes the usual comment upon Lydgate as the poet who 'adournyd our tong.'[5] He has high hopes of the possibilities of the language as compared with contemporary vernaculars, considering it

[1] *A Comedy concernynge thre lawes* (1538), sig. D. iii^v.
[2] *Terens in englysh* (1520), sig. A. i^r.   [3] *Ibid.*   [4] *Ibid.*   [5] *Ibid.*

EARLY TUDOR DRAMA

> amplyfyed so
> That we therin now translate as well may
> As in eny other tongis other can do.[1]

Passing to the question of the vocabulary of the English language, he asserts that

> In englysh many wordys do habound
> That no greke nor laten for them can be found,[2]

a bold assertion in an age which tended to deplore the poverty of the vernacular as compared with the rich resources of the classical languages. He thinks that

> the cause that our tong is so plenteouse now[3]

is that

> we kepe our englysh contynually
> And of the other tongis many wordis we borow
> which now for englysh we vse & occupy.[4]

Whether or not this account of linguistic practice is accurate, it is at least important that a man so keenly interested in the welfare of the English language was handling drama. Satisfaction with the language was the stimulus to creation in the vernacular and has

> gyuen corage gretly
> To dyuers & specyally now of late
> To them that this comedy haue translate.[5]

The Prologue ends with a plea addressed particularly to the learned, who tend to underrate the powers of the vernacular as compared with the languages of scholarship. Rastell aims at the entertainment and instruction of the wider audience and begs the learned

> to take no dysdayn
> Though this be compylyd in our vulgare spech
> yet lernyng therby some men may attayn.[6]

The Rastell family was closely connected with Sir Thomas More[7] and this conscious endeavour to promulgate the cause of vernacular language and literature is therefore made

[1] *Terens in englysh* (1520), sig. A. ii[v].   [2] *Ibid.*   [3] *Ibid.*   [4] *Ibid.*   [5] *Ibid.*   [6] *Ibid.*
[7] For the relations of the Rastell circle with Sir Thomas More see A. W. Reed, *Early Tudor Drama* (1926).

EARLY TUDOR CRITICISM

under the auspices of English scholarship and progressive thought. So serious is the purpose of this group concerning the future of the drama in English that, some time before 1526, John Rastell built a theatre in his 'ground beside Finsbury.'[1] This theatre was to provide for the presentation of plays written with the aim of educating ordinary people with no particular literary training. It is a practical justification of the importance of English drama. The work of Rastell and his collaborators was intended to be both an example of what could be achieved and an incentive to further translation and creation in the English language. The Messenger in the interlude of *The Four Elements* is Rastell's mouthpiece, explaining how he

> in his mynde hath oft tymes ponderyd
> What nombre of bok[s] in our tong maternall
> Of toyes and tryfellys be made and imprynted
> And few of them of matter substancyall
> For though many make bok[s] yet vnneth ye shall
> In our englyshe tonge fynde any mark[s]
> Of connynge that is regardyd by clerk[s].[2]

Rastell's work is undertaken in a spirit specifically critical. He examines the literature which is his heritage and makes a conscious attempt to reconcile it with the needs of a new age, bringing to bear upon the mediaeval form a new seriousness of literary purpose. Rastell, of course, was not More, still less was he Erasmus, yet there remains an element of paradox in the juxtaposition of the unwieldy, even uncouth, moral interlude with one so closely connected with a humanist circle. Rastell's faithfulness to the native form is a significant proof of its vigour and adaptability to contemporary purposes. That he continues to use it shows that he was sure of its continued appeal to the audience whom he wished to reach. Rastell is conscious of the stirring of new life in his age, when

[1] See A. W. Reed, *op. cit.*, pp. 230–233.
C. R. Baskerville, 'John Rastell's Dramatic Activities,' in *Modern Philology*, 1916, p. 189.
[2] *A new interlude and a mery of the nature of the iiii. elements* (1519), sig. A. ii^r.

> euery man after his fantesye
> Wyll wryte his conseyte be it neuer so rude
> Be it vertuous vycyous wysedome or foly.[1]

This readiness to write needed the purpose and direction given by a serious literary aim and an appraisal of language in the light of all the new discussion concerning the vernacular. Rastell is sure that the language is adequate

> ... yf clerk[s] in this realme wolde take payn so
> Consyderyng that our tonge is now suffycyent
> To expoun any hard sentence euydent,[2]

both in creative work, and in translation into 'englyshe well correct and approbate.'[3]

Rastell's addressing of his work to the unlearned leads him, as it leads the translators, to consider the kind of language to be used and to the same rejection of the ornate style lest it should obscure the meaning. Therefore it is not

> with rethoryk ... adournyd
> For perhappis in this matter muche eloquence
> Sholde make it tedious or hurt the sentence.[4]

The rapidity with which the native drama reflects the tastes and opinions of the age shows that it was no obsolescent mediaeval survival but a plastic and sensitive form. When men of the calibre of the Rastells deem it worthy of a place in vernacular literature and use it as a channel for the dissemination of their critical opinions concerning the English language, it makes an important contribution to the growth of literary and linguistic awareness in the Early Tudor period.

While these changes and developments were taking place in the native drama, in academic circles the infiltration of classical precept and study was becoming perceptible. The plays of Plautus and Terence were being revived and acted. College accounts show that Terence was being acted as

---

[1] *Ibid.*, A. ii^v. [2] *Ibid.*, A. ii^r. [3] *Ibid.*, A. ii^v. [4] *Ibid.*, A.iv^v.

EARLY TUDOR CRITICISM

early as 1510.[1] In 1536 Aristophanes' *Plutus* was acted at St. John's in Greek[2] and his *Pax* at Trinity in 1546.[3] Study of classical drama in the light of classical precept was part of the stimulating teaching of Sir John Cheke at Cambridge and he and the group of scholars associated with him discussed

> the preceptes of *Aristotle* and *Horace De Arte Poetica*, with the examples of *Euripides, Sophocles and Seneca*.[4]

From critical study of their models, these men turn to the writing of imitative work, usually in Latin, which is judged by the same canons. Of these first attempts Ascham says:

> ... not one I am sure is able to abyde the trew touch of *Aristotle's* preceptes, and *Euripides* examples, saue onely two, that euer I saw, M. *Watsons Absalon*, and *Georgius Buckananus Iephthe*.[5]

Although it is at first confined to the Latin drama, criticism, in the sense of the application of the canons of antiquity and the study of classical examples, is beginning to be active.

The relation of drama to moral edification still remains strong, limiting the conception of the aim and effect of tragedy to the didactic. The general attitude is that explained by John Christopherson in the 'Carmina' following the dedicatory epistle to *Jepthes* (1546 or 1555–6?), the only English academic play in Greek known to have survived:

> Proinde nos portenta quaeque immania
> Reiecimus, Dei seculi Oracula.
> Materia suppetit hinc Tragoediae proba.
> Hinc clara licet exempla vitae promere
> Ergo labores hic locandos duximus,
> Virtutis vbi decorus elucet nitor.[6]

Martin Bucer in the *De Regno Christi* (1550) left a critical document relative to the study of University drama at this

[1] See G. C. Moore Smith, *College Plays performed in the University of Cambridge* (1923), p. 4.
[2] *Ibid.*   [3] *Ibid.*   [4] *Scholemaster*, p. 284.   [5] *Ibid.*
[6] Quoted by F. S. Boas, *University Drama in the Tudor Age* (1914), p. 48.

time. It includes a discourse upon the benefits of tragedy to the morals of youth. He says that

> proprium est tragoediae, quae ad certam morum correctionem, & piam conferat vitae institutionem.[1]

The excessively restricting result of this moral attitude is shown in his desire to limit material for tragedy to the lives of saints, prophets and apostles with Scriptural foundation. These, he says, have an immediately beneficial effect:

> Quae omnia cùm mirificam vim habeant fidem in Deum confirmandi, & amorem studiumque Dei accēdendi, admirationem item pietatis atque iusticie, & horrorem impietatis, omnisque peruersitatis ingenerandi atque augendi; quanto magis deceat Christianos, vt ex his sua poemata sumant....[2]

It is obvious that the Aristotelian conception of tragedy has as yet made no headway.

Although such stress is laid upon the treatment of religious subjects, the miracle play ready to their hands is never considered by these scholars as containing any germs of dramatic conception. As vernacular drama and the common entertainment of the people it was beneath their notice. It is never admitted as a *genre* of drama and is seldom even called *comoedia* or *tragoedia*.

The classical meaning of these terms had suffered an eclipse in the Middle Ages. It is a commonplace of literary history that these names were applied to narrative of any kind, and distinguished the directions or curves of the action. Events working to a solution provided the material of comedy; a *peripateia* from greatness to misery made the stuff of tragedy. The definition of tragedy in Chaucer's *Monk's Tale* is succinct and representative of the mediaeval conception of

> a certeyn storie,
> As olde bokes maken us memorie,
> Of him that stood in greet prosperitee

[1] Quoted *Ibid.*, p. 65.   [2] *Ibid.*, p. 66.

EARLY TUDOR CRITICISM

And is y-fallen out of heigh degree
Into miserie, and endeth wreechedly.[1]

Similarly for comedy the conception was of a narrative in elegiac verse with a 'happy' ending. The Lives of the Saints or the tales of Walter Map could be included within its scope. The currency of this idea was promoted by the use of Ovid as a model of narrative in the schools and, as Ovid was accounted a comic writer, his versified tales become models for this type of narrative. Lydgate's comment on Chaucer as the writer of 'fressh commedies'[2] and one who also 'sometyme made full pitous tragedies'[3] comprehends both definitions.

The use of the terms in the Renascence marks a recognition of them as denoting *genres* purely dramatic, as exemplified in the work of Terence and Plautus, Sophocles, Euripides and Seneca. When Elyot speaks of

Therence and other that were writers of comedies,[4]

the classical form is definitely recognized. When the terms are so used at an early date we have a proof of 'Renascence' outlook, existing not yet in the age but in individuals. The looser use persists. Seven years later, John Bale applies the term still in its mediaeval sense to a mystery play with a prosperous ending, speaking of

A brefe Comedy or Enterlude of Iohan Baptystes preachynge in the wildernesse. (1538)[5]

Some approximation of the two uses seems to be indicated in a definition in the Preface to Nicholas Udall's translation of Erasmus' *Apophthegms*. 'Comedies' are there called 'merie entreludes,' in the sense that the aim may be entertainment, as contrasted with 'tragedies,' meaning 'sadde entreludes, whiche wee call staige plaies.'[6]

[1] *The Canterbury Tales*, ed. W. W. Skeat (1894), 'The Monk's Prologue,' p. 243, ll. 3163–3167.
[2] *Fall of Princes*, ed. H. Bergen, E.E.T.S. (Extra Series, No. 121), 1924, p. 7, ll. 246–248.
[3] *Ibid.* [4] *Gouernour*, Vol. 1, p. 123. [5] See *Harleian Miscellany*, Vol. 1, 1744.
[6] *Op. cit.*, Preface of Erasmus.

EARLY TUDOR DRAMA

The acceptance of a *genre* 'comedy' or plays of a purely entertaining nature, was delayed because the allegorical habit persists strongly, particularly in the morality form. Nicholas Udall is conscious of the long moralizing tradition behind him:

> The wyse Poets long time heretofore,
> Vnder merrie Comedies secretes did declare,
> Wherein was contained very vertuous lore,
> With mysteries and forewarnings very rare.[1]

The gradual emergence of comedy as a piece of dramatic artifice with no deep meaning essential to its mirth-making purpose is, nevertheless, traceable in this period. Udall knows

> nothing more comēdable for a mās recreation
> Than Mirth which is vsed in an honest fashion.
> For Myrth prolongeth lyfe, and causeth health.
> Mirth recreates our spirites and voydeth pensiuenesse, ...[2]

as seen in *Ralph Roister Doister* itself. Similarly the author of *Jack Juggler*, whether or not he was Nicholas Udall,[3] delights

> to make at seasuns cōueniēt pastims mirth and game.
> As he hath dō this matter nor woorth an oyster shel;
> Except percace it shall fortune too make you laugh well.
> And for that purpose onlye this maker did it write, ...[4]

The mid-century farce, *Gammer Gurtons Nedle*, the sole representative of vernacular University comedy in England, achieves this purely entertaining end without any of the paraphernalia of classical allusion or elaborate language. Diccon the buffoon is made to comment on this absence of learned elements:

---

[1] *Ralph Roister Doister* (1552), ed. W. W Greg, *Malone Society Reprints*, 1934 (1935), Prologue, sig. A. ij, ll. 16-19.
[2] *Ibid.*, ll. 6-9.
[3] See Introduction to edition of *Jack Jugeler* by W. H. Williams (1914).
[4] *Jack Juggler*, ed. 3, prepared by B. Ifor Evans and W. W. Greg, *Malone Society Reprints*, 1936 (1937), Prologue, ll. 61-64.

EARLY TUDOR CRITICISM

A man I thyncke myght make a playe
And nede no worde to this they saye
Being but halfe a Clarke.[1]

The shift of emphasis away from preoccupation with latent instructional purpose is assisted by the increasing attention to the technique of play construction. The tendency grows to conceive of the drama as a literary species with its own rules. The imposition of these upon the material to hand may show a constructive attempt to endow even homiletic and didactic material with the local habitation and name proper to the dramatic form. The curious hybrid form known as the 'Christian Terence,'[2] attempting to reconcile the Christian allegory with the classical technique, is an outcome of this critical attitude to structure.

While Terence serves as the model for comedy, Seneca serves a similar purpose for tragedy. In academic circles at least there may have been some germ of critical study of Seneca before the sixteenth century. As early as the late fourteenth and early fifteenth centuries, the English Dominican and scholar, Nicholas Treveth, produced a body of discussion about the work of Seneca including *In Declamationes Senecae* and *In Tragoedias Senecae*. He taught in the schools at Oxford on his return from the Continent where he was connected with scholarly circles, but, although he may have passed on some knowledge of the work of Seneca, such knowledge became intermittent later. 'Senek full soberly with his tragediis' appears in Skelton's *Garlande of Laurell*,[3] and is named by Ascham as having had a place in the discussions of the Cambridge circle. He is adjudged inferior to the great Greek tragic writers. When he is considering the books

---
[1] *Gammer Gurtons Nedle*, ed. H. F. B. Brett-Smith, *Percy Reprints*, No. 2 (1920), Act 2, sc. ii, ll. 10–12, p. 23.
[2] See *Studies in the Literary Relations of England and Germany in the Sixteenth Century*, C. H. Herford (1886), p. 79.
[3] *Op. cit.*, Vol. 1, p. 376, l. 358.

EARLY TUDOR DRAMA

most worthie for a man, the louer of learning and honestie, to spend his life in,[1]

Ascham finds Seneca less worthy of inclusion than the Greeks:

> In Tragedies (the goodliest Argument of all, and for the vse, either of a learned preacher, or a Ciuill Ientleman, more profitable than *Homer, Pindar, Virgill,* and *Horace*: yea comparable in myne opinion, with the doctrine of *Aristotle, Plato,* and *Xenophon,*) the *Grecians, Sophocles* and *Euripides* far ouer match our *Seneca,* in *Latin,* namely in οἰκονομια *et Decoro,* although *Senecaes* elocutiō and verse be verei commendable for hys tyme.[2]

This pronouncement is the result of careful and critical comparison of the relative merits of Greek and Latin drama. The preference for the Greek tragedy indicates discrimination, a perception of the true worth of high tragedy as against the elaborate devices and highly stylized speech which appealed so strongly to dramatists in the latter half of the Tudor period. The Cambridge Circle demonstrates, in the examination of the drama as in other controversies, the soundness of its critical methods.

As educationalists, Elyot and Ascham inevitably lay stress upon the use of the drama to convey important lessons of ethics and conduct. In a sense, therefore, the didactic trend of dramatic purpose is reinforced by them at the same time as the more literary study of technique and critical principles is growing up. The importance of the drama in their schemes of the learning necessary to a man of balanced culture helps to establish it, however, as worthy of serious consideration.

Elyot considers that tragedy becomes particularly important

> whan a man is comen to mature yeres, and that reason in him is confirmed with serious lerning and longe experience.[3]

The effect upon such a man will be that he will profit from the lessons contained in it. He will

[1] *Scholemaster,* p. 275. [2] *Ibid.,* p. 276. [2] *Gouernour,* Vol. 1, p. 71.

EARLY TUDOR CRITICISM

execrate and abhorre the intollerable life of tyrantes. and shall contemne the foly and dotage expressed by poetes lasciuious.[1]

Elyot lays stress in the definitions of comedy and tragedy contained in his *Dictionary* (1538) upon the imitation of life contained in these forms of literature. *Tragoedia* he defines as

> an enterlude, wherin the personages do represent somme hystorie or fable lamentable, for the crueltie and myserye therin expressed.[2]

Comicus is a 'maker of enterludes'[3] and *comoedus* 'a player in enterludes.'[4] The function of Comedy he understands as the exposition of the lower levels of life:

> an enterlude, wherin the common vices of men and womenne are apparently declared in personages.[5]

He expands the latter definition elsewhere, describing comedy as

> a mirrour of man's life, wherin euell is nat taught but discouered; to the intent that men beholdynge the promptnes of youth unto vice, the snares of harlotts and baudes laide for yonge myndes, the disceipte of seruantes, the chaunces of fortune contrary to mennes expectation, they beinge therof warned may prepare them selfe to resist or preuente occasion.[6]

He meets the obvious argument that this representation of evil in comedies may be conducive to evil by pointing out that

> by the same argument nat onely entreludes in englisshe, but also sermones, wherin some vice is declared, shulde be to the beholders and herers like occasion to encreace sinners.[7]

The Aristotelian definition that drama consists in the representation of 'men in action' is taken literally by the Renascence interpretation of the doctrine of imitation. Ascham includes his discussion of the drama in the topic *Imitatio*, for

> of this *Imitation* writeth *Plato* at large in 3 *de Rep.*[8]

and follows his source in regarding 'the whole doctrine of

---
[1] *Gouernour*, Vol. 1, p. 71. [2] *Bibliotheca Eliotae*, 1545 edition, sig. Dd^r.
[3] *Ibid.*, sig. Co^v. [4] *Ibid.* [5] *Ibid.* [6] *Gouernour*, Vol. 1, pp. 124–125.
[7] *Ibid.*, p. 126. [8] *Scholemaster*, p. 266.

142

EARLY TUDOR DRAMA

Comedies and Tragedies' as a 'perfite imitation, or faire liuelie painted picture of the life of euerie degree of man,'[1] a definition which was attributed to Cicero on the authority of Donatus.

The work of Plautus and Terence is used extensively in this period, to inculcate the pure Latinity upon which scholars of the Renascence period insisted. Critical study of the diction becomes necessary in the reading of these plays. Plautus especially is esteemed

> for that purenesse of the Latin tong in Rome, whan Rome did most florish in wel doing, and so thereby, in well speaking also,

and he is

> soch a plentifull storehouse, for common eloquence ... as the Latin tong ... hath not the like agayne.[2]

The diction of Terence is 'pure and proper'[3] and

> his wordes, be chosen so purelie, placed so orderly, and all his stuffe so neetlie packed vp, and wittely compassed in euerie place, as, by all wise men's iudgement, he is counted the cunninger workeman, and to haue his shop, for the rowme that is in it, more finely appointed, and trimlier ordered, than Plautus is.[4]

The study of style in Plautus and Terence ensures their work a place in the curriculum of the grammar school and of private education. Nicholas Udall collects his *Floures for Latyne Speakynge* (1553) from Terence and Terence's *Andria* is translated into English as early as 1520. The result of this wide study is the creation of an audience familiar with classical form and style, a preparation for the gradual adoption of classical form into vernacular drama.

This transference of classical criteria to the vernacular forms imposes a stricter framework upon the somewhat amorphous morality and checks the tendency towards the purely narrative form. Elyot in his *Dictionary* (1538) recognizes *actus* as 'the partes of a commedy or playe'[5] and

[1] *Scholemaster*, p. 266.   [2] *Ibid.*, p. 287.   [3] *Ibid.*, p. 288.   [4] *Ibid.*, p. 287.
[5] 1545 ed., sig. A^v.

143

EARLY TUDOR CRITICISM

by the time of *Gammer Gurtons Nedle* and *Gorbuduc* the act and scene division of classical drama is evident in both comedy and tragedy in English. There is at this date no body of critical work in England as there was in Italy[1] discussing the technique of drama with reference to these divisions or to the so-called 'Three Unities.' There must be, in spite of this reluctance to formulate opinion, some critical perception and decision behind the completeness of a play such as *Ralph Roister Doister* as behind the work of Wyatt and Surrey, where it is similarly inarticulate. *Ralph Roister Doister* carefully preserves the Unities of Place, Time and Action, and uses many of the classical verbal devices, ingenuity and *sticomuthia*. *Gammer Gurtons Nedle*, a purely native product, has the same studied framework, although the vigorous presentation of character is very far from the conventionalized classic treatment.

The appearance of work written in accordance with classical precept and example proves the existence of a conscious application of rules and methods derived from antique models. The slowness of the spread of these newly recovered literary ideals is due in part to the restriction of such knowledge by its very nature to academic circles, who were disinclined to acknowledge the status of English drama. Critical discussion *per se* is limited mainly to the Latin drama composed by University men in imitation of the classics. That they should leave such little evidence of opinions which must have bulked large in their discussions may be ascribed to the recurring English trait—the lack of any impulse among writers to form a 'school' to lay down rules of composition. The scholars were not the national poets nor the arbiters of the taste of the people.

The results of the study of, and commentary upon, classical drama as a branch of classical literature were at first felt only by scholars. They used texts printed abroad with

[1] See J. E. Spingarn, *History of Literary Criticism in the Renaissance* (Columbia University Studies in Comparative Literature), 1908, pp. 60–106.

EARLY TUDOR DRAMA

all the additional material added by foreign editors and men of letters. They travelled to centres of learning in Europe and were drawn into the main channels of ideas. The impulse was, therefore, to make use of all this scholarly knowledge and apparatus by creation in the language of scholarship. Discussion of critical theory in the Early Tudor period must involve a study of the purely academic drama, which was usually accompanied by explanatory preface or comment.

The aim and effect of tragedy are discussed by John Christopherson in the 'Carmina' following the Dedicatory Epistle to *Jephthes* (*c.* 1545). Tragedy moves the spectators by the grandeur of style and gravity of matter, having effect rather upon their mind and will than deeply stirring emotion according to the Aristotelian καθάρσις. He says:

> ... Attamen Tragicae Camoenae maximū
> Decus merentur propter ornatū styli.
> Graecibus enim verbis refertae permovent
> Animos, theatrū tristibus complent modis./
>
> Sententiis crebris fluunt in intimos
> Sensus. Voluptatē afferunt spectantibus.
> Oculis subijciunt flexilē aeui tramitem
> Illustrium casus acerbos exprimunt.[1]

Since the effect is to be moral elevation, the subject matter of tragedy must be selected for its edifying value and the choice of these writers of academic tragedy in Northern Europe falls upon Scriptural episode. Christopherson bears out Bucer's pronouncement:

> Priscis in hoc primas Poetis deferunt
> Nisi quod Tragoediā expleant mendacijs
> Res ficta, verba splendida, stylus elegans,
> Procul tamen syncera veritas abest
> Proinde nos portenta quaque immania
> Reiecimus, Dei seculi Oracula.
> Materia suppetit hinc Tragoedia proba.
> Hinc clara licet exempla vitae promere.

[1] Quoted F. S. Boas, *op. cit.*, pp. 47-48.

EARLY TUDOR CRITICISM

Ergo labores hic locandos duximus,
Virtutis vbi decorus elucet nitor.[1]

Bucer elaborates this decision farther, urging the use of Biblical material alone because

> ... omnia cùm mirificam vim habeant fidem in Deum confirmandi, & amenem studiumque Dei accēdendi, admirationem item pietatis atque iusticie, & horrorem impietatis, omnis que peruersitatis ingenerandi atque augendi: quanto magis deceat Christianos, vt ex his sua poemata sumant, quibus magna & illustra hominum consilia, conatus, ingenium, affectus atque casus repraesentent quàm ex impijs ethnicorum vel fabulis vel historijs.[2]

The result of this preoccupation is to divert attention from the recovered technical aspects which produced such a spate of critical work in Italy. Scholarship in Northern Europe was turned to purposes primarily moral rather than aesthetic. The development of literary criticism of the drama in England is therefore retarded. France and Italy readily accepted the ideas distilled from Aristotle and Horace, while England found the mediaeval habit of relating literature to other motives, especially the theological, more to her taste and reinforced this conception with the results of the Revival of Learning.

There is, then, in this Early Tudor period no systematic discussion of the methods and precepts of dramatic theory. The attitude of writers of this time must be reconstructed from incidental comment and explanation and from the principles which seem to be inherent in the work itself.

The study of rhetoric, which touched upon so many aspects of style and composition in the Early Tudor period has some bearing also upon the drama. The theory of *decorum*, which had at first a purely stylistic application, was developed throughout the Early Tudor period, until, with the renewed neo-classical influence after the time of Sidney, it becomes one of the main tenets of dramatic composition. In the Early Tudor period it was not so firmly

[1] Quoted F. S. Boas, *op. cit.*, p. 48.   [2] *Ibid.*, p. 66.

EARLY TUDOR DRAMA

established. Sir Thomas Wilson discusses the choice of words appropriate to the style and matter chosen in his *Arte of Rhetorique*:

> Suche are thought apt wordes, that properly agre vnto that thyng, whiche thei signifie, and plainly expresse the nature of the same. . . . In weightie causes, graue wordes are thought moste nedefull, that the greatnesse of the matter, maie the rather appere in the vehemencie of their talke. So likewise of other, like order muste be taken. . . .[1]

Infringement of the rules of stylistic *decorum* lays the writer open to the charge of committing many faults of style. One of these, according to Richard Sherry,

> is when lighte and tryfling matters, are set out with gaye and blasing wordes. Suche as in Commedies are wont to be spoken, of crakyng souldiers & smell feastes.[2]

Since the dramatist must use a great variety of style and character and weld all the elements into a harmonious whole, the rules of rhetoric impinge very closely upon his work. For this reason, Nicholas Grimald's tutor, John 'Aerius',[3] in his criticism of *Christus Redivivus* (1541) attributes the achievement of an effect of unity to the skill of one 'experienced in the art of oratory.'[4]

The work of Nicholas Grimald indicates the existence in Oxford, as in Cambridge at the time of Cheke, of a careful study of the rules of dramatic composition, derived partly from the study of rhetoric and partly from the study of classical and neo-classical doctrine. Grimald, writing his tragi-comedy, *Christus Redivivus*, at the age of twenty is aware of a critical background, of the conscious craftsmanship required for literary composition, of the value of

---

[1] fol. 88r.
Cf. Aristotle, *Rhetorica*, Bk. 3, vii. 24: 'Style will have propriety, if it is pathetic, characteristic, and proportionate to the subject. This proportion means that important subjects shall not be treated in a random way, nor trivial subjects in a grand way. . . .' (Translated R. C. Jebb, ed. J. E. Sandys, 1909, p. 159.)
[2] *Op. cit.*, fol. xr.
[3] See *The Life and Poems of Nicholas Grimald*, L. E. Merrill. (Yale Studies in English, 169) 1925, p. 101, Note 6.
[4] *Ibid.*, Dedicatory Epistle to *Christus Redivivus*. See p. 109 for the Latin.

words and of stylistic *decorum*. He is most explicit on the standards by which he is working. He says,

> ... I feared in no small degree that there would be those who would very justly complain that I could not set forth this event properly, and clothe so great a theme in appropriate diction. I know, of course, that, as in everyday life and conduct, it is considered especially difficult to perceive and note in each instance what is proper[1]—a subject that is learnedly treated by philosophers in their ethical teachings—so in poetical compositions, to fashion diction in harmony with the matter and characters demands a man of keen insight, of refined judgment, unusual diligence and blessed with great leisure.[2]

The juxtaposition of 'keen insight' and 'refined judgment' implies some recognition of a critical discipline such as that to which Horace ascribes such importance:

> scribendi recte sapere est et principium et fons.[3]

Poetic composition is a conscious art requiring the exercise of the critical faculty to accompany creation:

> natura fieret laudabile carmen an arte
> quaesitum est: ego nec studium sine divite vena
> nec rude quid prosit video ingenium; alterius sic
> altera poscit opem res et coniurat amice.[4]

Grimald discusses also the question of the propriety of diction, the precept derived from the rhetoricians which was hardened into the rule of *decorum* in the full development of neo-classical doctrine during the Renascence and applied to all kinds of literary composition. The emotion to be expressed influences the choice of diction, for the same style cannot be employed

> in plain, straightforward narrative as in thrasonical boasting; in soothing consolation as in complaint; in a voice from heaven as in the wailings that arise from hell.[5]

---

[1] Cf. Horace: *Ars Poetica*.
    ... tantum series iuncturaque pollet,
    tantum de medio sumptis accedit honoris.
ll. 242, 243 (ed. E. H. Blakeney, 1928, p. 27).
[2] *Op. cit.*, pp. 95, 97. See pp. 94–96 for the Latin. [3] *Op. cit.*, p. 34, l. 309.
[4] *Ibid.*, ll. 408–411, pp. 37–38. [5] *Op. cit.*, for the Latin, p. 96.

EARLY TUDOR DRAMA

It is an essential quality of the orator's art that he should be able to use a speech appropriate for every occasion. Cicero says,

> Nam cum est oratio mollis et tenera et ita flexibilis ut sequatur quocumque torqueas, tum et naturae variae et voluntates multum inter se distantia effecerunt genera dicendi[1]

and applies the rule to poetical composition also:

> Πρέπον appellant hoc Graeci, nos dicamus sane decorum: de quo praeclare et multa praecipiuntur et res est cognitione dignissima, huius ignoratione non modo in vita sed saepissime et in poematis et in oratione peccatur. Est autem quid deceat oratori videndum non in sententiis solum sed etiam in verbis....[2]

The quality of τον Πρέπον is explained by Aristotle:

> Passion is expressed, when an outrage is in question, by the language of anger; when impious or shameful deeds are in question, by the language of indignation and aversion; when praiseworthy things are in question, by admiring language; when piteous things, by lowly language—and so in the other cases.[3]

Quintilian rates this rhetorical requirement highly, stressing the importance of appropriate diction as essential to every composition and the consequent disaster

> si genus sublime dicendi parvis in causis, parvum limatumque grandibus, laetum tristibus, lene asperis, minax supplicibus, summissum concitatis, trux atque violentum iucundis adhibeamus?[4]

This makes for variety of style, the diversity of tone and emotion by which an orator can sway his audience and by which poetry of all kinds may move its readers similarly. Grimald knows this classical precept well and says that

> ... the work ought to be done so in accordance with the nature, the change, and the manner of the action, that at one time the verse may creep along in an unpretentious measure, shunning, as it were, the adornments and forms of oratory,

---

[1] *Orator*, XVI. 52, ed. A. S. Wilkins (1903).   [2] *Ibid.*, XXI, 70.
[3] *Rhetorica*, III, vii, 2, *op. cit.*, p. 159.   [4] *Op. cit.*, Bk. 11, 3.

EARLY TUDOR CRITICISM

whereas at other times it may speed along in a fuller and more pretentious course. Often, however, with marshaled words in battle array, it makes an onset like the snowstorms of winter, and its eloquence bursts forth unchecked, and gains the fields in which it can revel.[1]

He has also absorbed the Horatian doctrine whereby the rule of propriety is made to apply minutely to all characteristic details such as emotion, social status, age. He says, for instance, that

> it is certain that one and the same sort of style is not called for in the case of a rich man as of a poor one.[2]

Horace insists that well-known characters shall have always their significant attributes[3] and that there shall be a speech suitable for the old man and for the youth:

> aetatis cuiusque notandi sunt tibi mores,
> mobilibusque decor naturis dandus et annis.[4]

Quintilian has the same rule:

> Ipsum etiam eloquentiae genus alios aliud decet[5]

and, by this rule, the character remains consistent throughout:

> si quid inexpertum scaenae committis et sudes
> personam formere novam, servetur ad imum
> qualis ab incepto processerit.[6]

As regards the framework of the drama, there is manifest acquaintance with the so-called 'Unities,' which are comprehended in the reference of Grimald's tutor to the harmony of 'theme, time . . . place.'[7] The 'Unity of Action' derives from the Aristotelian dictum that the action of a tragedy shall have beginning, middle and end and be complete in itself.[8] Horace echoes this precept:

> . . . sic veris falsa remiscet,
> primo ne medium, medio ne discrepet imum,[9]

[1] *Op. cit.*, for the Latin, see p. 97.
[2] See *op. cit.*, p. 96, for the Latin.
[3] *Op. cit.*, p. 26, ll. 119–124.
[4] *Ibid.*, p. 28, ll. 156–157.
[5] *Op. cit.*, Vol. 5, p. 172.
[6] Horace, *op. cit.*, ll. 125–126.
[7] *Op. cit.* See p. 108 for the Latin.
[8] *Poetics.* I 450.b.2.
[9] *Op. cit.*, p. 28, ll. 151–152.

and adds his own technical injunction that the structure shall consist of five acts:

> neve minor neu sit quinto productior actu
> fabula, quae posci vult et spectata reponi.[1]

Grimald follows Horace in adopting the five-act division, but, while accepting this, repudiates the rigid restriction of the time of the action to twenty-four hours[2] which Aristotle derived from contemporary stage practice and which Italian critics interpreted variously.[3] Grimald feels it necessary to comment upon his disregard of this unity and tries to account for it by citing a precedent in Plautus. Reporting the opinions of his tutor, he says:

> Likewise, he concluded that the scenes were not so far apart but they could easily, and without trouble, be reduced to one stage-setting; and that, if any one is surprised, either because I have united in one and the same action a story covering several days, and different periods of time, or because such a pleasing close is given to such a mournful and lamentable beginning, he ought to understand that I follow Plautus, whose play, the Captivi, above all, is represented as taking place during an interval of several days, and passes moreover from a sad beginning to a happy ending.[4]

It is clear that Grimald was conversant with the principles of classical dramatic criticism. The remarkable fact is that he chose to work independently of them. He speaks of the *decorum* used in the portrayal of character but disregards its extension to distinguish between the *genres* of comedy and tragedy. This extension is particularly clear in Horace and Cicero. Horace says:

> versibus exponi tragicis res comica non vult
> indignatur item privatis ac prope socco
> dignis carminibus narrari cena Thyestae,[5]

allowing for variety only occasionally:

[1] *Ibid.*, p. 29, ll. 189-190.   [2] *Op. cit.*, p. 21.
[3] See J. E. Spingarn, *op. cit.*, pp. 91-93 for discussion and comparison.
[4] *Op. cit.* See p. 110 for the Latin of Grimald.   [5] *Op. cit.*, p. 25, ll. 89-91.

EARLY TUDOR CRITICISM

> interdum tamen et vocem comoedia tollit,
> iratusque Chremes tumido delitigat ore;
> et tragicus plerumque dolet sermone pedestri
> Telephus et Peleus. . . .[1]

Cicero clearly distinguishes *genres* of literature not to be mingled:

> Oratorum genera esse dicuntur tamquam poetarum; id secus est, nam alterum est multiplex. Poematis enim tragici comici epici melici etiam ac dithyrambici, quo magis est tractatum [a Latinis], suum cuiusque est, diversum a reliquis. Itaque et in tragoedia comicum vitiosum est et in comoedia turpe tragicum. . . .[2]

Grimald's tragi-comedy, on the other hand, earns the commendation of his tutor because of the variety of elements within it, for

> great things had been interwoven with the small, joyous with sad, obscure with manifest, incredible with probable. Moreover, just as the first act yields to tragic sorrow, in order that the subject-matter may keep its title, so the fifth and last adapts itself to delight and joy; likewise, in order that variety may be opposed to satiety, in all the other intermediate acts sad and cheerful incidents are inserted in turn.[3]

In these passages from Grimald and his tutor variety of tone and subject matter in one work are justified mainly by the efficacy of the mixture and by appeal to a rhetorical *decorum* regarding only the matching of occasion and speaker with appropriate words. These views offer a significant contrast with those of Sir Thomas More earlier and Sir Philip Sidney later. As early as 1516, More includes in his *Utopia* a reference to the principles of *decorum* governing dramatic usage. He does not relate them to the *schole philosophie*[4] but to the wider code of *decorum* governing both life and literature,

---

[1] *Ibid.*, p. 25, ll. 93–96.
[2] *De Optimo Genere Oratorvm*, I. i, ed. A. S. Wilkins (1903).
[3] *Op. cit.* See p. 108 for the Latin.
[4] *The Utopia of Sir Thomas More: in Latin from the edition of March 1518, and in English from the first edition of Ralph Robynson's translation in 1551*, ed. J. H. Lupton, 1895, p. 97.

an other philosophye more cyuyle, whyche knoweth as ye wolde saye her owne stage, and thereafter orderynge and behauynge herselfe in the playe that she hathe in hande, playethe her parte accordynglye wyth comlynes, vtteringe nothynge owte of dewe ordre and fassyon.[1]

According to the dictates of this sense of the fitness of things he condemns the mingling of comedy and tragedy and the incongruity which would result if

> whyles a commodye of Plautus is playinge . . . yowe shoulde sodenlye come vpon the stage in a philosophers apparrell, and reherse owte of Octauia the place wherin Seneca dysputeth with Nero. . . .[2]

The 'tragycall comedye or gallymalfreye'[3] seems to More to violate, not only the rules of drama, but a universal principle.

More than fifty years later Sidney criticizes 'this mongrell Tragicomedie.'[4]

Between these two *loci critici* at the beginning and end of the sixteenth century, Grimald stands for a more liberal view, in his acceptance of the hybrid which both More and Sidney condemned as inadmissible. His choice is amply justified by the variety of drama in the full Elizabethan period, the triumphant product of the vigorous native tradition tempered but not inhibited by the usage and precedent of foreign and classical models.

---

[1] *Ibid.*, p. 98. [2] *Ibid.* [3] *Ibid.*, p. 99.
[4] *Defence of Poesie* (printed 1595), ed. A. Feuillerat (1923), p. 39.

CHAPTER VIII

MISCELLANEOUS: IRONY AND PARODY; THE NEW COURTLY POETRY

THE end of a literary tradition is frequently marked by the production of burlesque and parody. The ridicule of worn-out symbols by their use in a mocking context is one of the most effective methods of criticism. It implies a two-fold process—thorough mastery and understanding of the literary *genre* involved, to make the imitation convincing and complete in itself, and the faculty to examine and assess it from a detached point of view. The two stages, in fact, constitute a critical judgment.

It has been seen that the fifteenth century was a period of re-adjustment, of the gathering of new energy and therefore prone to examine the literary forms which were handed on from the preceding generations. In the sixteenth century the situation was complicated by new forces and the need for a survey of literary and linguistic problems became more acute, as a prelude to the time when the fervour of creation should become too tense to allow of any detachment. The progress of this critical activity is in England quickened by the acute insight and balanced moderation of Erasmus and Thomas More. Their easy adoption of the satirical and detached point of view may owe something to their interest in the work of Lucian. About 1506, they collaborated in a translation into Latin of some of his dialogues,[1] at the same time stimulating each other and catching a spark of Lucian's spirit. They provide the subtle exposure of excesses by means of the oblique method of irony. Erasmus in his *Praise of Folly* (1509) caricatures and condemns the failings of his age. More suggests improvements by his picture of the ideal state of *Utopia* in a more constructive spirit. In *The Praise of Folly* the reader

[1] *Luciani . . . cōplura opuscula . . . ab Erasmo Roterodame & Thomas Moro . . . in Latinorum lingua traducta.*

IRONY AND PARODY

shall soon espie, how in euery mattier, yea almost every clause, is hidden besides the myrth, some deaper sence and purpose.[1]

The follies Erasmus exposes are comprehensive of many fashions, literary and learned. At a time when the creation of Latin work in strict imitation of the ancients had become so fervid a fashion that it threatened to stifle originality and creative impulse, Folly calls such verses

> most balde, and foolisshe, but never the more faile thei of some as verie asses as they, who will hieghly commende the same: whiche putteth theim in suche a flusshe, as plainly they beleeve they haue recovered Virgiles owne vaine in poetrie.[2]

She comments upon the linguistic fashion for aureate and elaborate speech, derived from rhetoric in its worst sense, 'full of sound and fury, signifying nothing' and not related to the clear, careful and appropriate language advocated by Quintilian.

She smiles at the vanity of human learning:

> For this is truely not the least of my pleasant propretees, to make men ever sette moste store by straunge and outlandisshe thyngs.[3]

Logicians and men who argue with excessive tortuousness in the manner of the 'schools' are included in Folly's skipping survey. She rejects their elaborate method of setting out a subject and will not

> accordyng to these common Sophisters and Rhetoriciens maner, go about to shew by diffinicion what I am, and muche lesse use any division.[4]

This seems to accord with Thomas More's significant comment on the learning of the Utopians:

> But as they in all thynges be almoste equall to our olde auncyente clerkes, so our newe Logiciens // in subtyll inuentyons haue farre passed and gone beyonde them. For they haue not deuysed one of all those rules of restryctyons, amplytycatyons, and supposytyons, very wittelye inuented in the small

---

[1] Chaloner, 'To the Reader,' *op. cit.*, p. v. [2] *Ibid.*, p. 46.
[3] *Ibid.*, pp. 3–4. [4] *Ibid.*, p. 3.

Logycalles, whyche heare oure chyldren in euerye place do learne.[1]

This is a hint of the acrimony felt by men of the humanist persuasion for the schoolmen, upon which Francis Bacon commented. Looking back to find the causes of the decay of learning, he finds this feud to be a turning point in the intellectual development of the sixteenth century. He says that at this early time:

> . . . the ancient authors, both in divinity and in humanity, which had long time slept in libraries, began generally to be read and revolved. This by consequence did draw on a necessity of a more exquisite travail in the languages original wherein these authors did write, for the better understanding of those authors and the better advantage of pressing and applying their words. And thereof grew again a delight in their manner and phrase, and an admiration of that kind of writing; which was much furthered and precipitated by the enmity and opposition that the propounders of those (primitive but seeming new) opinions had against the schoolmen; who were generally of the contrary part, and whose writings were altogether in a differing style and form; taking liberty to coin and frame new terms of art to express their own sense and to avoid circuit, without regard to the pureness, pleasantness, and (as I may call it) lawfulness of the phrase or word. . . .[2]

Poets as well as 'rhetoricians' and logicians draw a shaft from Folly, although she admits that they

> are somewhat lesse beholding unto me, not withstandyng, evin by theyr profession they shew theim selves to be of my secte, a free kynde of men, that lyke peincters maie feigne what they list, whose studie tendeth naught els, than to fede fooles eares with mere trifles and foolisshe fables.[3]

Erasmus by his irony subtly detaches the foolish element in every branch of study at which Folly tilts. As Chaloner says,

> And seeyng the vices of our daies are suche as cannot enough

[1] Op. cit., pp. 184–185.
[2] The Advancement of Learning. The Works of Francis Bacon, ed. Spedding, Ellis, Heath (1876), Vol. 3, p. 283.   [3] Op. cit., p. 47.

IRONY AND PARODY

be spoken against, what knowe we, if Erasmus in this booke thought good betweene game and ernest to rebuke the same?[1]

More rebuilds the picture of the world of ideas drawn by Erasmus, showing by significant stress where he considers the failings of his own age to lie. As regards intellectual activity, he is emphatic about the value of Greek studies. Of Raphaell Hythlodaye, the traveller, he says that he

> is verye well lerned in the Latyne tonge; but profounde and excellent in the greke tonge, wherein he euer bestowed more stuyde than in the lattyne, because he had geuen hym selfe holye to the studye of Philosophy.[2]

Implied in this is the humanist recognition of the value of the originals, the new zest for deriving knowledge from the fountain head. He praises the aptitude of the Utopians for learning Greek, since

> in lesse than iii. yeres space their was nothing in the Greke tonge that they lackede. They were able to reade good authors wythout anny staye, if the booke were not false.[3]

Textual study gave Renascence scholars distaste for mutilated and inaccurate texts. It was a branch of criticism which grew up and flourished, as the preliminary to exact and authentic knowledge.

Erasmus and More thus by indirections find directions out, the former by the obliquity of irony and the latter by the reconstructive idealism in which the spirit of criticism has performed its preliminary task of detachment and dissection.

Hints of parody enable us to trace changes of feeling for mediaeval forms during the Early Tudor period. Chaucer in the fourteenth century slyly mocked the romance by a *reductio ad absurdum* in *Sir Thopas*, exploiting the critical possibilities of the burlesque imitation. The poets of the Early Tudor period, similarly alert to criticism, were quick to use the same method. The *Bowge of Courte*, which is an example of Skelton's treatment of allegory, may also be re-

[1] *Ibid.*, p. iv. [2] *Op. cit.*, p. 27. [3] *Ibid.*, p. 214.

lated more particularly to the tradition of the 'Ship of Fools.' 'Fool literature' had a long tradition throughout the Middle Ages.[1] In England, Wincker's *Speculum Stultorum* (thirteenth century) and Lydgate's *Order of Fools*[2] had classified and portrayed the kinds of human folly, Wincker in lively vein, Lydgate more drearily. On the eve of the Northern Renascence the fool-device was vigorously exploited in Sebastian Brandt's *Narrenschiff* (1494), its translation into Latin by Locher (1497) and its English translation by Alexander Barclay in *The Ship of Fools* (1508). In the work of Barclay there is no pervasive tone of irony or hint of self-conscious imitation. It is written with stern moral earnestness and is intended to castigate the vice of the world by its severe exposure. There is more humour and vigour in *Cocke Lorelles Bote*[3] and its closeness to reality removes it slightly from allegorical and moral edification into the realm of satire, the more pungently critical *genre*. Skelton, by temperament not content with the abstract, confirms the use of this ship-and-fool framework for satirical purposes and writes his *Bowge of Courte*, of which 'Desire' says:

> Fortune gydeth and ruleth all oure shyppe.
> Whome she hateth shall ouer the see boorde skyp.[4]

He describes the haunt of rascals with vividly characteristic traits instead of dull abstractions. He is, therefore, in making this new use of the old tradition, examining and criticising its resources. *The Tunnyng of Elynour Rummyng* (before 1509?) with its Hogarthian procession of vagabonds and wastrels, shows Skelton passing wholly into the realm of realism which had been approached by the author of *Cocke Lorelles Bote*, and contemplating the extent and kinds of human folly.

[1] See Enid Welsford, *The Fool* (1935).
[2] See C. H. Herford, *The Literary Relations of England and Germany in the Sixteenth Century* (1886), pp. 325–326.
[3] Author unknown. Date probably early in the reign of Henry VIII. See edition by J. P. Edmond (1884), reprinted from a unique copy printed by Wynkyn de Worde.
[4] *Op. cit.*, Vol. I, p. 34, ll. 111–112.

THE NEW COURTLY POETRY

The poets of the Early Tudor period did not seize upon the mediaeval romance for laughter and parody as quickly as might have been expected. For a long time it remained the literature of pastime and entertainment, fit first for the aristocracy, as in Caxton's time, and later for the literate public which has always had a taste for light fiction. The poets' surveys of their reading nearly always include a list of romances. In the pageant of lovers who pass before the poet's eyes in Gavin Douglas' *Palice of Honour*, Palamon and Arcite have their place with Dido and Aeneas, Troilus and Cressida, Paris and Helen.[1] Palamon and Arcite appear again in Skelton's list,[2] and many more figures of romance are mentioned with them:

> ... rede haue I
> Of Gawen and syr Guy, ...[3]
> Of Arturs rounde table,
> With his knightes commendable,
> And dame Gaynour, his quene, ...[4]
>
> Of Trystram and kynge Marke,
> And al the hole warke
> Of Bele Isold his wyfe,
> For whom was moch stryfe; ...[5]
>
> And of syr Lybius,
> Named Dysconius;
> Of Quater Filz Amund,
> And how they were sommonde
> To Rome, to Charlemayne, ...[6]

Skelton's erudition seems no less impressive in romance reading than in the study of the classical authors.

From the fourteenth century onwards there is a slight tone of disparagement in the judgments of poets upon the triviality of the romance. Chaucer slyly suspends belief in saying of the *Nonnes Preestes Tale*,

---

[1] *Op. cit.*, Vol. 1, p. 22, ll. 25-28. [2] *Phyllyp Sparowe, op. cit.*, Vol. I, p. 70, l. 616.
[3] *Ibid.*, ll. 628-629. [4] *Ibid.*, ll. 634-636. [5] *Ibid.*, ll. 641-644.
[6] *Ibid.*, p. 71, ll. 649-653.

EARLY TUDOR CRITICISM

This storie is al-so trewe, I undertake,
As is the book of Launcelot du Lake,
That wommen holde in ful gret reverence.[1]

He nevertheless accepted the romance for pageantry as in the *Squire's Tale*, for chivalrous love as in the *Knight's Tale* and for the apotheosis of love and its tragic development as in *Troilus and Criseyde* which originally 'grew up out of the French Romantic school.'[2]

Chaucer's successors began to mock the highly idealized conventions of romantic love. Occleve's lady is described in terms which reduce the tradition to the ridiculous. He anticipates the description of Bottom the Weaver as Thisbe's love, and says,

> Of my lady, wel me reioise I may.
> hir golden forheed is ful narw & smal;
> hir browes been lyk to dym reed coral;
> And as the Ieet / hir yen glistren ay,[3]

and his mock eulogy continues with a coarseness which is the antidote to the highly spiritualized and conventionalized portraits of the mediaeval romance.

Chaucer's Scottish successors in the late fifteenth and early sixteenth centuries are openly scornful of the traditions of the romance. William Dunbar uses his Goliardic genius to mock chivalric usage. He uses the setting of the mediaeval tournament for a jousting that

> Lang befoir in hell wes cryid,
> In presens of Mahoun;
> Betuix a tel3our and ane sowtar,
> A pricklouss and ane hobell clowttar,
> The barress wes maid boun.[4]

Sir David Lyndsay has a similar tournament 'betuix James Watsoun and Jhone Barbour, servitouris to King James the Fyft':

[1] Ed. W. W. Skeat, *op. cit.*, p. 282, ll. 4401–4403.
[2] W. P. Ker, *Epic and Romance* (1908), p. 368.
[3] *Hoccleve's Humorous Praise of his Lady*. *Poetical Works*, ed. Gollancz, E.E.T.S. (Original Series 83), 1925, Vol. 2, p. 37, ll. 1–7.
[4] *The Turnament. Poetical Works*, ed. J. Small (1893), Vol. 2, p. 122.

THE NEW COURTLY POETRY

> James was ane man of greit intelligence,
> Ane medicinar ful of experience;
> And Jhone Barbour, he was ane nobill leche.[1]

Gavin Douglas uses the term in a clearly depreciatory context. When the man of his dream begins to read

> all the mowis in this mold, sen God merkit man,[2]

Douglas dismisses his offer

> Thir romanis ar bot rydlis, quod I to that ray.[3]

On the whole, the poets of the Early Tudor period do not advance as far as open criticism of the romance. Stephen Hawes' re-modelling of the chivalrous romance and his incorporation of a discourse on the Seven Liberal Arts constitute a tacit admission that the form could not be passed unchanged into the Tudor period, but he is by temperament too romantically inclined to scoff at it. Caxton, like Malory, had tried to recall the gentlemen of England to the chivalry of a passing phase of society.[4] He published *The Book of the Ordre of Chyualry* to furnish the canons of knighthood, *Kyng Arthur* for an example and information about the figure

> whyche ought moost to be remembred emonge vs englysshe men tofore al other crysten kynges,[5]

adducing much evidence for the existence of King Arthur against sceptics.[6] He prints also *Godefroy of Bologne* (1481), *The Book of the Knyght of the Towre* (1484), *The Fayttes of Armes* (1489) and *Blanchardyn and Eglantine* (1489) to support the demand for romance and stories of knighthood.

The popularity of this literature seemed to Tudor writers of more serious purpose to menace the study of serious works.

---

[1] *Poetical Works*, ed. D. Laing (1879), Vol. 1, p. 125.
[2] *Op. cit.*, Vol. 3, p. 147, l. 12.   [3] *Ibid.*, l. 21.
[4] 'O ye knyghtes of Englond where is the custome and vsage of noble chyualry that was vsed in tho dayes/ . . . rede the noble volumes of saynt graal of lancelot / of galaad / of Trystram / of perse forest / of percyual / of gawayn / & many mso / Ther shalle ye see manhode / curtosye & gentylnesse.'
William Caxton, *The Book of the Ordre of Chyualry*, from a French version of Ramón Lull's *Le Libre del Ordre de Cauayleria*, A. T. P. Byles, E.E.T.S. (1926), p. 122, ll. 8–16.
[5] Prologue, *op. cit.*, p. 92.   [6] *Ibid.*, pp. 93–94.

EARLY TUDOR CRITICISM

William Tyndale is even afraid that it may deflect attention from the reading of the Bible and resents the prohibition of the reading of the Scriptures when facilely entertaining literature is freely allowed. He maintains

> that this thretenynge and forbiddynge the laye people to reade the scripture is not for love of youre soules (which they care for as t*h*e foxe doeth for *th*e gysse) is evide*n*te & clerer the*n* the sonne / in-as-moch as they permitte & sofre you to reade Robyn hode & bevise of ha*m*pto*n* / hercules / hector, a*n*d troylus, with a t[h]ousande histories & fables of love & wa*n*tones & of rybaudry as fylthy as herte ca*n* thinke / to corrupte t*h*e myndes of youth with all / clene co*n*trary to the doctrine of christ & of his apostles.[1]

Roger Ascham is of the same mind that reading of romances, far from instilling noble knightly ideals, is definitely harmful:

> In our fathers tyme, nothing was red, but bookes of fayned cheualrie, wherin a man by redinge, shuld be led to none other ende, but onely to manslaughter & baudrye.//Yf any man suppose they were good ynough to passe the tyme with al, he is deceyued. For surelye vayne woordes doo worke no smal thinge in vayne, ignoraunt, and younge mindes, specially yf they be gyuen any thynge thervnto of theyr owne nature.[2]

He refers to the years past when romances were very widely read, particularly the

> *Morte Arthure:* the whole pleasure of which booke standeth in two speciall poyntes, in open mans slaughter, and bold bawdrye.[3]

He says that he remembers the time

> when Gods Bible was banished the Court, and *Morte Arthure* receiued into the Princes chamber.[4]

In the Renascence period the desire to relate literature to the useful purpose of improving character and personality by example and instruction had become stronger. The literature of antiquity was studied for its civilizing qualities

[1] *Obedience of a Christien man*, sig. C iiii^r.
[2] *To All Gentle Men and Yomen of Englande*, prefixed to *Toxophilus*, pp. xiv-xv.
[3] *Scholemaster*, p. 231.   [4] *Ibid.*

THE NEW COURTLY POETRY

and any literature which could not be related to this high purpose was condemned as harmful to character and morals. It was clear that the age of mediaeval chivalry was past and that the desire to resuscitate its codes and standards was an ineffectual attempt to reinstate an anachronism. The chivalric world of the Middle Ages was giving place to a new conception of the 'gentleman,' which was to have its own effect upon the literary production and conception of the sixteenth century.

For the hero of mediaeval chivalry is substituted the courtier, who was to be a man of culture and of intellectual as well as physical attainments, joining 'learnyng with cumlie exercises.'[1] The most comprehensive survey of the requirements of the courtier is the work cited by Ascham,[2] Castiglione's *Il Cortegiano*, translated by Sir Thomas Hoby in 1561. One of the courtier's most necessary gifts is that of

> writinge both rime and prose, and especiallye in this our vulgar tunge.[3]

This writing must be more than a mere literary exercise. It must be founded upon real knowledge and strenuous attention must be paid to excellence of style and diction. Castiglione insists that

> the principal mater and necessary for a Courtyer to speak and write wel, I beleve is knowledge. For he that hath not knowledge and the thing in his minde that deserveth to be understood, can neither speak nor write it. Then must he couch in a good order that he hath to speake or to write, and afterward expresse it wel with wordes; the which (if I be not deceived) ought to be apt, chosen, clere, and wel applyed, and (above al) in use also among the people.[4]

This attitude makes for a certain re-instatement of vernacular literature and an encouragement to creation in the social strata which had easiest access to all the wealth of classical literature through training, either under such tutors as Elyot, or at the Universities where there was the stimulus of

[1] *Ibid.*, p. 218.   [2] *Ibid.*   [3] *Op. cit.*, p. 85.   [4] *Ibid.*, pp. 69–70.

men such as Cheke. The writing of poetry became an accomplishment to be desired in a courtier.

Castiglione's book had extensive influence in England, but there was no original work in English which gave so comprehensive a system for the making of the scholar-courtier except perhaps Elyot's *Gouernour*. The *Institucion of a Gentleman* (written 1555, printed 1568) has not so wide a scope. Its author includes learning in the necessary accomplishments of a gentleman, but does not discuss the point. He says:

> Thys gentleman for the further ornature and setting furth of hys person, ought to be learned, to have knowledge in tounges, and to be apte in the feates of armes, for the defence of his cuntrey.[1]

Even this brief mention shows how the conception was accepted in England and there are two courtier-poets who are its incarnation.

Sir Thomas Wyatt and Henry Howard, Earl of Surrey, moved in courtly circles where literature was held in high esteem. Fired by Italian ideals, they devoted attention to poetry as a serious art, while bringing to it the care for deftness and polish demanded by its courtly audience. Their importance in English literary achievement of the sixteenth century is largely due to this combination of serious purpose and conviction of the possibilities of the English language, with the taste for form and style which led them to supplement English resources with foreign models. Poetry regains its prestige in the hands of such 'Courtly makers'[2] and becomes of value for its expression of personal emotion, as distinct from the allegorical bias of the mediaeval period.

The technical aspects of the verse of Wyatt and Surrey have been fully dealt with by specialists.[3] It has been estab-

---

[1] Reprinted by Charles Whittingham, 1839. (No pagination.)
[2] George Puttenham, *The Arte of English Poesie*, Chap. 31, ed. G. D. Willcock and A. Walker (1936), p. 61.
[3] E.g. A. K. Foxwell, *A Study of Sir Thomas Wyatt's Poems* (1911).
  E. M. W. Tillyard, *The Poesy of Sir Thomas Wyatt: a selection and a study* (1929).
  E. K. Chambers, *Sir Thomas Wyatt and some Collected Studies* (1933).
  F. M. Padelford, *The Poems of Henry Howard, Earl of Surrey* (University of Washington Publications, Language and Literature. Vol. 1) 1920.

THE NEW COURTLY POETRY

lished that Wyatt owed much to Marot and Saint-Gelais after 1530,[1] and that he also made use of the Italian modifications of the Provençal stock upon which the French poets drew.[2] English prosody owes to him the introduction of the sonnet form, derived from Petrarch with modifications,[3] of the 'terza rima,' derived from Alamanni, and 'ottava rima,' from Serafino.[4]

That this introduction of foreign metres was made in a critical spirit, which did not disregard the vigorous genius of his native tongue, is proved by Wyatt's sensitive care for the English language. His study of Chaucer seems to have led to his recovery of the secret of the final '-e,'[5] the loss of which had impaired the understanding of Chaucer's metre and crippled English verse.[6] Poems in the English 'rhyme royal' and 'poulter's measure' stand among his poems on foreign models and the close connection between native and foreign strains is shown by many poems with native structure and content of foreign ideas.[7] He uses pure, direct English, free from archaism or affectation, which approximates closely to the standards set up by Castiglione, who insists that a courtier

> shall have a good grace, and especially in speaking, if he avoide curiositye.[8]

Wyatt with his Italian contacts must have absorbed many of these ideals. Such scanty evidence of his convictions as is traceable bears out this impression. In the short preface to his translation of Plutarch's *De Tranquillitate Animi* he consciously declares his choice of the plain style and his love of brevity:

> It shall seme harde vnto the parauenture gentyll reder / this trāslation / what for shorte maner of speche / and what for dyuers straunge names in the storyes. As for the shortenesse aduyse it wele and it shalbe the plesaunter / when thou vnderstandest it.[9]

---

[1] See A. K. Foxwell, *op. cit.*, pp. 64 ff.   [2] *Ibid.*, p. 69.   [3] *Ibid.*, pp. 82–86.
[4] *Ibid.*, pp. 86–87.   [5] *Ibid.*, p. 38.
[6] See G. Saintsbury, *Manual of English Prosody* (1910), pp. 161–163.
[7] See E. M. Tillyard, *op. cit.*, pp. 14–15.   [8] *Op. cit.*, p. 62.
[9] *Op. cit.*, To the reder.

EARLY TUDOR CRITICISM

Like Wyatt, Surrey experimented with a variety of metres both foreign and English. His chief contribution to English prosody is blank verse in his translation of the Aeneid.[1] His diction, like that of Wyatt is pure and firm, with a sprinkling of Chaucerian terms to lend a judicious flavour of the archaic.

In an age when English versification was loose and the choice of diction a burning question, Wyatt and Surrey impose discipline upon the form and clarifying perception of language on the content. They make English poetry more flexible and capable of expressing many varied emotions by the range of feelings which they covered. It might be said of them both, as Surrey said of Wyatt, that they had

> A hand, that taught what might be sayd in ryme;
> That reft Chaucer the glory of his wit;
> A mark, the which—vnparfited, for time—
> Some may approche, but neuer none shall hit

in the Early Tudor period.[2] Their work proves the vitality of the age, its readiness to adopt whatever could augment and support its own achievement without surrendering its essentially sturdy and independent character.

The prestige of these men contributed to the defence of poets and poetry against the accusations of falsehood and frivolity perennially brought against them by zealots and utilitarians. The lines of attack and defence as they run through Sidney,[3] Harington[4] and others are already sketched by Elyot:

> For the name of a poete, wherat nowe, (specially in this realme,) men haue such indignation, that they use onely poetes and poetry in the contempt of eloquence, was in aunciente tyme in hygh estimation.[5]

Behind the shield of Wyatt and Surrey, other poets could gather, as is proved by the collection of the *Songes and*

---
[1] See Surrey's *Fourth Boke of Virgill*, ed. Herbert Hartmann (1933).
[2] *A Third Tribute to Wyatt*, see F. M. Padelford, *op. cit.*, p. 81, No. 46.
[3] *Apologie for Poetrie* or *Defence of Poesie*, printed 1595, written before 1583.
[4] Preface to *Orlando Furioso in English heroical verse*, by J. Haringtō (1591).
[5] *Gouernour*, Vol. I, pp. 120–121.

THE NEW COURTLY POETRY

Sonettes, written by the ryght honorable Lorde/Henry Howard late Earle of Sur-/ rey, and other./ Apud Richardum Tottel./ 1557.[1] Their position as innovators was recognized by Puttenham[2] and their first editor links them to the patriotic movement for the improvement of English, saying that by comparison with the work of

diuers Latines, Italians, and other[3]

these poets show that

our tong is able in that kynde to do as praiseworthely as y[e] rest,[4]

and he therefore publishes them

to the honor of the Englishe tong.[5]

Their success in combining innovation (from foreign models) and tradition (in their faith in the English language and literature) at a particularly difficult turning point in our literary history must rest upon strong and clear, though silent, critical perceptions.

From the early 'fifties onward the *Mirror for Magistrates* was looming on the horizon.[6] With this, in spite of the discipleship to Boccaccio and Lydgate, we step into a mid-Tudor world. Its most distinguished contributor, however, the young Thomas Sackville,[7] wrote as the inheritor of the traditions described here. His few significant critical touches show us the poet becoming explicit and serve to round off this survey. The recently discovered manuscript of

---

[1] Edited H. E. Rollins (Harvard University Press, 1928).
[2] '... hauing trauailed into Italie, and there tasted the sweete and stately measures and stile of the Italiā Poesie as nouices newly crept out of the schooles of *Dante Arioste* and *Petrarch*, they greatly pollished our rude & homely maner of vulgar Poesie...' *op. cit.*, p. 60.
[3] *The Printer to the Reader*, ed. Rollins, Vol. I, p. 2.   [4] *Ibid*   [5] *Ibid*.
[6] See Marguerite Hearsey. *The Complaint of Henry, Duke of Buckingham, including the Induction or, Thomas Sackville's contribution to the Mirror for Magistrates.* (Yale Studies in English, Vol. 86), 1936, p. 1, Note 1.)
The actual plan seems to have been conceived in 1554. See Miss Hearsey, *op. cit.*, p. 10, and W. F. Trench, *The Mirror for Magistrates; its Origin and Influence* (1898. Privately printed.)
[7] Sackville was born in 1536. 'MS. Harley. 757, fol. 127, gives his age at the inquisition taken at the death of his father, in 1566, as twenty-nine.' R. W. Sackville-West, *The Works of Thomas Sackville* (1839), p. iv. Quoted by Miss Hearsey, *op. cit.*, p. 22, Note 12.

EARLY TUDOR CRITICISM

the *Complaint of Henry, Duke of Buckingham*, reveals the poet in his work-shop jotting down ideas as they suggest themselves, trying variant versions and generally testing and examining his creation. Wyatt and Surrey take their place with Ovid and Chaucer in the background of tradition to which he refers, Wyatt for 'his sacred psalmes'[1] and for

>   al the plaintes wherin he wrote his pain
>   when he lay fetterd in the fyry chain
>   of cruell love.[2]

Sackville engages in the tradition of deprecation with a zest which shows how eagerly he has studied his authorities, but it does not come glibly from his pen. He remembers a passage in Lydgate which may help him, and writes the memorandum:

>   Loke in the prologue of Bochas fol. lxiii.[3]

He weighs the relative values of ways of working in the conventional classical allusions:

>   I neuer lened to Helicon so mayny floods as part Brittain part me from it. . . .[4]

or

>   I never drank of pernasus spring. . . .[5]

or the simple statement:

>   mine eloquens is rudeness.[6]

or, reverting to the classical:

>   I have no fresh licour out of the conduictes of Calliope.[7]

and

>   I haue no flowers of rethoricke through Clio.[8]

Then come more naive memoranda:

---

[1] Published 1549, *Additional Lines*, 31, ed. M. Hearsey, *op. cit.*, p. 90.
[2] *Ibid.*, *ll.* 39–41.
[3] *Ibid.*, l. 68. The passage to which he refers is traced by Miss Hearsey to *The Tragedies of Ihon Bochas of all such princes as fell, etc.* (*c.* 1555), 'a copy of which is to be found in St. John's College Library (Cambridge).' Notes in Commentary, p. 123.
[4] *Additional Lines*, l. 69.   [5] *Ibid.*, l. 70.   [6] *Ibid.*, l. 74.
[7] *Ibid.*, l. 75.   [8] *Ibid.*, l. 76.

THE NEW COURTLY POETRY

> note the ix muses dwel with Citherea on parnaso.[1]

and:

> remember M*agister* Burdeus? promise for the showing of Senecas chore? touching the captation of auram popularem.[2]

These jottings are eloquent of the self-consciously critical fervour for which the Early Tudor period provides so strenuous and attentive a preparation.

---
[1] *Ibid.*, l. 77.   [2] *Ibid.*, ll. 87–89.

CONCLUSION

MORE than one section of this book has expressed appreciation of the vigour and scope of the Early Tudor period. Wherever possible, efforts have been made to allow the age to speak for itself, at least to remember when writing of it the mental horizon by which every spokesman of the period was necessarily limited. In particular an attempt has been made to avoid making of 'Humanism' a Procrustes' bed by which to measure the value and interest of the age to which belong the vitality of Skelton, the sturdiness of the Interlude, the zeal, half-scholarly, half partisan, of the Bible translators, the shrewd good sense of Caxton.

Though change is continuous, the turn from one order to another is, of course, particularly important in the first half of the sixteenth century. The Early Tudor period has acquired the label 'Age of Transition.' What gives particular interest to the juxtaposition of old and new in the reign of Henry VIII is the fact that changes in literary and scholarly direction came to a country where the 'native' tradition had itself undergone a kind of renascence and found vigorous and appropriate means of presenting the contemporary world and where, moreover, energy and resolution had already gathered about at least one critical topic. Controversy was rife in the world of letters as elsewhere and consequently decisions had to be made by every writer. Thus opinions which might have remained unformulated had to be tested and strengthened to meet public challenge, and from these arguments and discussions grow the principles which belong to criticism.

It has been shown that the Early Tudor period inherited plenty of material which comes under the order of 'static' criticism. The systems of grammar and rhetoric preserved throughout the Middle Ages the habit of judging language, of considering its appropriateness in the several literary

CONCLUSION

forms. In the light of the manuscripts recovered by fifteenth and sixteenth century scholars in Italy this knowledge was augmented and modified until the term 'rhetoric' came to embrace most matters of linguistic interest. The variety of meanings attached to the word in the Early Tudor period shows how rapidly interest in language was changing and developing. To Hawes and Berners it is the 'facundious' art, the gift of expressing thought in sweet sounds that give delight. Later it becomes to the scholarly Ascham the groundwork of criticism, of the appreciation of language and of the rules of craftsmanship governing topics such as the *genres* of literature and the nature of decorum. The 'arts of rhetoric' compiled by Sherry and Wilson are the nearest approach in Early Tudor literature to handbooks of literary and linguistic criticism. In the circles of Grimald and Ascham 'rhetoric' is a richly inclusive term. It comprises the greater part of what is later separated out as 'Literary Criticism' or 'Poetic.' Moreover, within this well-tilled field, principles and ideas proved not only discussable but assimilable, which, offered later as 'Poetic', made slower headway.

It was the partisan enthusiasm for language which provided the spark of energy which fires men of this period, unifies their many intellectual interests and gives life to their study of inherited learning. The result of this competitive energy is to transform the static into the dynamic; the traditional rhetoric is metamorphosed into the most keenly debated topic of contemporary criticism. There was rivalry between individuals, between *côteries* and between nations. The assertion of scholarly prowess, the championing and vindication of the vernacular to offset the claims, loudly voiced, of the other European countries, were the concern of every patriotic English man of letters, whether poet, dramatist or translator and of the new reading public. The passion for language was no artificial or pedantic revival. It has the vitality of judgments made independently of foreign or classical borrowing and proved upon the

EARLY TUDOR CRITICISM

pulses. The later Scaligerian and Italianate elements superimposed in the reign of Elizabeth were and remained more foreign. The way to criticism through language was proved in the Early Tudor period to be the natural and 'native' way. Men had begun to 'compt halfe a God ... such a one assuredly that can plainly, distinctly, ple[n]tifully, and aptly vtter bothe wordes and matter' and to see that such comprehension lies at the root of literary excellence.

INDEX

Ad Herennium, 118, 119 n
Advancement of Learning. See Bacon, Francis
Aeditio. See Colet, John
Aelfric, 103
Aeneid. See Virgil, 21
Alfred, King of England, 56
Andria. See Terence
'Antibossicon' controversy, 83
Apophthegmes, Erasmus'. *See* Udall, Nicholas
Aristotle, recovery of MSS. of *Rhetorica* and *Poetica*, 115; theory of tragedy studied at Cambridge, 136; decorum of speech, 149
Ars Poetica. See Horace
Arte of Rhetorique. See Wilson, Sir Thomas
Arte or Craft of Rhethoryke. See Cox, Leonard
Ascham, Roger, place among Tudor men of letters, 56; correspondence with Sturm, 61; background of the *Scholemaster*, 66; influence of Quintilian, 86; account of Cheke at Cambridge, 93; mention of Gardiner, 94; as champion of the vernacular, 96; *Scholemaster* quoted, 67, 69, 84, 88, 89, 97, 117, 120, 136; *Letters*, 78, 79, 94; *Toxophilus*, 96, 103, 104

Bacon, Francis, *Advancement of Learning*, 156
Bale, John, *Brefe comedy or enterlude of Johan Baptystes preachynge in the Wyldernesse*, 131; *Temptacyon of our Lorde*, 131; *God's Promises*, 131; *Thre Lawes*, 132; use of term 'comedy,' 138
Barclay, Alexander, use of classical pastoral, 6, translation of Sallust, 61; *Ship of Fools*, 158
Beauvais, Vincent de, 65
Becke, Edmonde, translation of *Two dyaloges* by Erasmus, 44, 48
Belges, Jean Lemaire de, 9
Bourchier, John, Lord Berners, 1, 9, 14, 15
Brandt, Sebastian, *Narrenschiff*, 158
Bucer, Martin, *De Regno Christi*, 136, 137, 145, 146

Burrant, Robert, *Preceptes of Cato*, 43
Castiglione, Baldassare, *Il Cortegiano*, translated by Sir Thomas Hoby, place in Tudor system of education, 60, 163; quoted 45, 46, 56, 73, 100, 103, 105
Castle of Knowledge. See Record, Robert
Caxton, William, early critical utterance in English, ix; praise of Skelton's translations, 5; discussion of linguistic judgment shown in Prologues and Epilogues, 7–14; place among translators, 56; transmission of rhetorical precept, 110; recall to chivalry, 161
Chartres, Bernard of, 65
Chaucer, Geoffrey, stabilization of language, xii, 7; Caxton's comment, 14; Skelton's comment, 19; Tudor fashion for Chaucerian speech, 98; knowledge of rhetoric, 111; definition of tragedy in the *Monk's Tale*, 137; burlesque imitation in *Sir Thopas*, 157; *Nonnes Preestes Tale*, 160; *Troilus and Criseyde*, 160
Cheke, Sir John, controversy concerning Bible translation, 33, 46; translation of gospels, 34; leadership of Cambridge circle of scholars, 56, 57, 61, 91–92; accounts by Ascham of his influence and teaching, 78, 89, 93, 94; Greek controversy, 94; contemporary praise for mastery of English language, 95; spelling system, 96; distrust of foreign borrowings in English language, 100, 114; interest in rhetoric, 114, 115; use of Aristotle's works, 116; study of drama, 136
Christopherson, John, *Jephthes*, 136, 145
Cicero, Marcus Tullius, *De Officiis* translated by Grimald, 51, 52, 81; *De Amicitia*, translated by John Harington the elder, 50, 53; Ciceronian controversy, 87–88, 90; *Orator*, 149; *Rhetorica*, 149; *De Optimo Genere Oratorum*, 152
Cocke Lorell's Bote, 158

173

INDEX

Colet, John, connection with St. Paul's School, 59; *Aeditio*, 81; friendship with Erasmus, 90
Confutacyon of Tyndale's answere. See More, Thomas, Saint
Convivio. See Dante
Cordier, Mathurin, claim for vernacular, 79
Cortegiano, Il. See Castiglione, Baldassare
Coverdale, Miles, linguistic sense, 37; method of comparative translation, 38; stimulus of foreign translations, 40
Cox, Leonard, *Arte or Craft of Rhethoryke*, 43 n; sources, 115, purpose, 116, scope, 123; place among Tudor rhetoricians, 116–117

Dante, *Convivio*, *De Vulgari Eloquentia*, *Divina Commedia*, 89
De Duplici Copia Verborum. See Erasmus
Demosthenes, Cheke's preference, 115; *Orations* first translated into English by Sir Thomas Wilson, 115
De Recta et Emendata Scriptione Linguae Anglicanae. See Smith, Sir Thomas
De Regno Christi. See Bucer, Martin
De Vulgari Eloquentia. See Dante
Dialogue concernynge heresyes. See More, Thomas, Saint
Dictionary. See Elyot, Sir Thomas
Doctrinal of Princes. See Elyot, Sir Thomas
Dolet, Etienne, *La Manière de bien traduire d'une langue en aultre*, 47, 48
Dorne, John, *Daybook*, 63
Douglas, Gavin, new developments in his poetry, 1; comments on verse translation and linguistic question, 19–21; opinion endorsed by Udall, 36; translation of *Aeneid* quoted, 20, 21, 55, 120; *Palice of Honour*, 159, 161
Du Bellay, Joachim, *Défense et Illustration de La Langue Françoyse*, 48, 49 n, 89, 100, 104, 105, 117, 127
Dunbar, William, linguistic comment, 111; mock chivalric usage, 160

Elyot, Sir Thomas, hopes for English language, 35; place among translators, 49, 56; use of Quintilian, 66; *A svvete and devovte sermon of holy saynt Ciprian*, 48–49; *Image of Governance*, 53, 57; *Knowledge that maketh a Wise Man*, 102; conception of the poet, 121; definitions of dramatic terms in *Dictionary*, 142, 143; *Doctrinal of Princes*, 49; *Gouernour*, 45, 52, 55, 59, 60, 61, 67, 68, 71, 74, 75, 77, 81, 109, 112, 122, 141, 166
Erasmus, Desiderius, Bible translation 29; *Two dyalogues*, 44; connection with European scholarship, 61; Hervet's comment, 44; educational theory, 67, 71, 74, 75–76, 77; lectures in Greek, 78; friendship with English scholars, 90; *Paraphrases upon the newe testament*, see Udall, Nicholas; *Praise of Folie* quoted, 69, 97, 100, 154, 155, 156; *De duplici copia verborum*, 115; collaboration with More, 154
L'Esclaircissement de la langue françoyse. See Palsgrave, John
Exhortacion to Young Men. See Lupset, Thomas

Floures for Latyne Speakynge. See Udall' Nicholas
Fool literature, 158
Fulgens and Lucrece. See Medwall, Henry
Fullonius, translation by Palsgrave, 82

Gammer Gurton's Needle, 139, 140, 144
Gardiner, Stephen, Bishop of Winchester, opposition to printing of Great Bible, 33; zeal for Latin, 34; quarrel with Cheke concerning Greek pronunciation, 94; Ascham's account, 94
Garland, John of, 119
Gloucester, Humphrey, Duke of, humane scholarship in his time, xi, 90
Googe, Barnabe, 6
Gouernour, The Boke called the. See Elyot, Sir Thomas
Grimald, Nicholas, translation of Cicero *De Officiis*, 51, 52, 81; *Christus Redivivus*, 147; discussion of dramatic theory, 148–153

Harington, John, the Elder, translation of Cicero *De Amicitia*, 50, 53
Hawes, Stephen, innovations in his work, 1–4; individual use of chivalric romance, 5, 161; opinions on language of poetry, 17; *Pastime of Pleasure* quoted, 1, 2, 3, 5, 15, 17, 110–111, 121

INDEX

Hervet, Gentian, translation of Erasmus' *De Immensa Dei Misericordia*, 44
Heywood, John, use of French dramatic models, 129; *Wytty and Wyttles*, 129; *Play of Love*, 130; *Play of the Weather*, 130; *Play called the Foure P P*, 130; *Johan Johan*, 130; *Proverbs*, 130
Hickscorner, 128
Higden, Ranulph, translation of *Polychronicon* by Trevisa, xi, xii
Hoby, Sir Thomas, Letter prefixed to *The Book of The Courtier*, 45. For quotations from *The Courtier*, see Castiglione, Baldassare
Horace, *Ars Poetica*, 121, 122 n; Compared with Quintilian, 123; use of precepts by Grimald, 148, 150, 151
Horman, William, master of Eton, 63; participation in 'Antibossicon' controversy, 83; *Vulgaria*, 69, 70, 74, 78, 81, 84, 85
Howard, Henry, Earl of Surrey, use of blank verse, 166; contribution to English poetry, 166–167; influence on Thomas Sackville, 168
Hrotsvitha, 125

Image of Governance. See Elyot, Sir Thomas
Institiucion of a Gentleman, 164
Institutio Oratoria. See Quintilian

Jack Juggler, 139
Jewel, John, Bishop of Salisbury, 113; *Contra Rhetoricam*, 114
Johan Johan. See Heywood, John

La Manière de bien traduire d'une langue en aultre. See Dolet, Etienne
Lily, William, association with Magdalen College School, 63; High Mastership of St. Paul's, 77
Linacre, Thomas, 90
Lollard Bible, 24–26, 35
Lucian, translation of *Dialogues* by More and Erasmus, 154
Lupset, Thomas, 91
Lupus, Servatus, 65
Lydgate, John, 15, use of 'aureate' language, 1; tradition of allegory, 15; Skelton's comment, 19; *Order of Fools*, 158
Lyly, John, 9
Lyndsay, Sir David, mock chivalric usage, 160–161

Magdalen College School, 59, 60, 63
Magnyfycence. See Skelton, John
Marlowe, Christopher, *Jew of Malta*, 128; *Tamburlaine*, 129
Marot, Jean, 9
Medwall, Henry, *Fulgens and Lucrece*, 129; *Nature*, 129
Melancthon, *Institutiones Rhetoricae*, 115
Mirror for Magistrates, 167
More, Thomas Saint, controversy concerning Bible translation, 26–32; *Dialogue concernynge heresyes*, 27, 28; *Confutacyon of Tyndale's answere*, 32; friendship with Erasmus, 90; *Utopia*, 63–64, 81, 152–153, 154, 155, 157; collaboration with Erasmus in translation of Lucian, 154

Narrenschiff. See Brandt, Sebastian
Nature. See Medwall, Henry
Newe boke of Presidentes, A. See Phaer, Thomas
Nicolls, Thomas, translation of Thucydides, 46, 50–51
Nonnes Preestes Tale. See Chaucer, Geoffrey

Occleve, Thomas, *Humorous Praise of his Lady*, 160
Ovid, 138

Palsgrave, John, claim for vernacular in education, 79–80, 82; Epistle prefixed to *L'Esclaircissement de la langue françoyse*, 102
Paraphrases vpon the newe testament, Erasmus'. *See* Udall, Nicholas
Pastime of Pleasure. See Hawes, Stephen
Paynell, Thomas, 44
Pecock, Reginald, opinion of language suitable for Bible translation, xiii; critical interest in language, xiv; *Donet*, 24; *Reule of Crysten Religion*, 24
Phaer, Thomas, *A newe boke of Presidentes*, 43, 44; *Regiment of Life*, 43 n, 46 n
Play of Loue. See Heywood, John
Play of the Wether. See Heywood, John
Play called the Foure PP. See Heywood, John
Plutarch, *De Tranquillitate Animi*, translated by Wyatt, 165
Polychronicon. See Higden, Ranulph
Pope, Sir Thomas, 77

INDEX

Praise of Folie. See Erasmus
Proverbs. See Heywood, John
Purvey, John, Prologue to Old Testament, 25, 40
Puttenham, George, *Arte of English Poesie*, 167

Quintilian, re-discovery of MSS, 66; Tudor revival of his conception of grammar, 65, 75; modification by Whittinton, 73; *Institutio Oratoria* quoted, 65, 73, 84, 85, 108 n, 109 n, 113 n. 114 n, 120 n, 123; influence on new study of rhetoric in Tudor period, 107, 112; influence on work of Ascham, 86

Ramus, Peter, protest against Aristotelianism, 66
Rastell, John, translation of *Andria*, 132; care for vernacular in Prologue of this play, 132, 133, 135; connection with Thomas More, 133; building of theatre, 134; *Four Elements*, 134
Record, Robert, *Castle of Knowledge*, 101
Regiment of Life. See Phaer, Thomas
Respublica, 131
Rule of Reason. See Wilson, Sir Thomas

Sackville, Thomas, contribution to *Mirror for Magistrates*, 167–169
St. George, mummer's play of, 126
St. Paul's School, 59, 77
Saintsbury, George, *History of English Criticism*, quoted, ix
Salisbury, John of, 65
Scholemaster, The. See Ascham, Roger
Sébillet, Thomas, 127
Seneca, mentioned by Skelton, 140; by Ascham, 140, 141; work discussed by Nicholas Treveth, 140
Seville, Isidore of, mentioned by Petrarch, x
Sherry, Richard, headmaster of Magdalen College school, author of rhetorical treatises, 63; transmission of rhetorical standards, 114; *Treatise of the Figures of Grammer and Rhetorike* quoted, 84, 97, 104, 112, 113, 147; sources, 115; scope of work, 123
Skelton, John, place among Early Tudor poets, 1, 3; retreat from allegory, 4–6; choice of style, 16–19; *Bowge of Courte*, 2, 4, 158; *Colyn Cloute*, 4, 19; *Garlande of Laurell*, 4, 5, 16, 18, 140; *Phyllyp Sparowe*, 17; *Speke, Parrot*, 4, 64–65; *Magnyfycence*, 128; *Tunnyng of Elynour Rummyng*, 158; praise of Chaucer, 19
Smith, Sir Thomas, contents of library 92; reputation at Cambridge, 95; *De Recta et Emendata Scriptione Linguae Anglicanae*, 96
Spenser, Edmund, 6
Squire's Tale. See Chaucer, Geoffrey
Stanbridge, John, progressive ideas on education, 58, 85; association with Magdalen College School, 63; circulation of his *Vulgaria*, 63, quoted 70
Strype, John, *Life of Sir John Cheke* quoted, 95
Sturm, Johannes, correspondence with Ascham, 61; teaching methods, 66, 89

Tamburlaine. See Marlowe, Christopher
Terence, *Andria* translated by J. Rastell, 132; plays acted at Universities, 132; emergence of 'Christian Terence,' 140; criticism of diction by Ascham, 143; source of Udall's *Floures for Latyne Speakynge*, 143
Thopas, Sir. See Chaucer, Geoffrey
Tottel, Richard, *Songes and Sonettes*, 167
Toxophilus. See Ascham, Roger
Treatise of the Figures of Grammer and Rhetorike. See Sherry, Richard
Treveth, Nicholas, 140
Trevisa, John, translation of Higden's *Polychronicon*, xi, xii
Troilus and Criseyde. See Chaucer, Geoffrey
Tyndale, William, controversy with More, 29–32; language of Bible translation, 34; distrust of romance reading, 162

Udall, Nicholas, conception of translators duty, 35; preface to translation of Erasmus, *Paraphrases upon the newe testament*, 36, 40–41, 45, 47; headmaster of Eton, 63; preface to translation of Erasmus' *Apophthegmes*, 53, 138; *Ralph Roister Doister*, 63, quoted, 139, structure, 144; comment on comedy, 138; *Floures for Laytne Speakynge*, 143

176

INDEX

Utopia. See More, Thomas Saint

Vinsauf, Geoffroi de, 111, 119

Virgil, comment by Gavin Douglas, 20; translation of *Aeneid*, 19–21

Vives, Jean Luis, visit to England, 61; *De Causis Corruptium Artium* 69; claim for vernacular, 79; aim of education, 86

Whittingham, William, 38, 39

Whittinton, Robert, tribute to Skelton's Latin work, 5; progressive element in Tudor education, 58; publication of *Vulgaria*, 63; 'Antibossicon' controversy, 83; *Vulgaria* quoted, 59, 60, 64, 72, 73; translation of Cicero, *De Officiis*, 82–83

Wilson, Sir Thomas, concern with English language, 35, 85; place among Tudor men of letters, 56, 60; praise of Cheke, 92–93; transmission of principles of rhetoric, 114; *Arte of Rhetorique* quoted, 93, 97, 98, 99, 101, 106, 109, 112, 113, 117, 118, 119, 123, 147, sources, 116, scope, 124; *Rule of Reason*, 45, 47; translation of Demosthenes' *Orations*, 52, 54

Wolsey, Thomas, educational system, 76

Wyatt, Sir Thomas, translation of Plutarch, 52–53; services to English poetry, 164–166; technical innovations, 165; choice of language, 165; influence on Thomas Sackville, 168

Wycliffe, John, 25, 26, 37

Wycliffite tract (anonymous), 23

Wytty and Wyttles. See Heywood, John